THE BIBLE STORY

VOLUME III

TRIALS AND TRIUMPHS

(From the Death of Nadab and Abihu to the Anointing of David)

The

BIBLE STORY

More Than Four Hundred Stories in Ten Volumes
Covering the Entire Bible From Genesis to Revelation

VOLUME THREE
Trials and Triumphs

BY ARTHUR S. MAXWELL

Author of *Uncle Arthur's Bedtime Stories, The Children's Hour With Uncle Arthur,*
The Secret of the Cave, etc.

•

PACIFIC PRESS PUBLISHING ASSOCIATION
Mountain View, California

Russ Harlan

CONTENTS

5

← PAINTING BY RUSSELL HARLAN   © 1954, BY REVIEW AND HERALD

Their Egyptian slavery and the hardships of
their wilderness wanderings were forgotten by
the children of Israel in this beautiful, fruitful
land of Canaan which God had given them.

Part III—Stories of the Days of the Judges

JUDGES 1:1-RUTH 4:22

Part IV—Stories of Samuel and Saul

1 SAMUEL 1:1-16:13

PART I

Stories of Israel in the Wilderness

(Leviticus 9:1-Numbers 20:29)

STORY 1

Two Naughty Boys

AFTER all that happened that day in front of the tabernacle, when Aaron and his sons were consecrated to the priesthood, you would surely think that those four boys would be the last ones in the camp to get into trouble.

Had not Moses himself washed them in front of everybody? Had not he put on them those beautiful, clean clothes? Had not they all laid their hands upon the bullock and the two rams, confessing their sins? Had not blood been placed on their ears, their right thumbs, and their right toes?

Yes, indeed. And they couldn't have gone through all this without knowing what it meant. And if they forgot, even for a moment, every time they looked at their father there were the words, "HOLINESS TO THE LORD."

They knew all right. They understood. Moses couldn't have made it more plain that God wanted them to be the best young people in the camp, an example to all the boys and girls who had come out of Egypt.

9

← PAINTING BY RUSSELL HARLAN   © 1954, BY REVIEW AND HERALD

Aaron, assisted by his four sons, was ordained high priest to serve the people of God in their journey toward the Promised Land. His wonderful garments were most glorious to behold.

To Nadab, Abihu, Eleazar, and Ithamar was given a very wonderful opportunity. The more you think about it, the more you will see how big it really was, and how much God expected of them. They were to be the spiritual leaders of the youth of Israel—young men of such spotless character and noble living that all the boys and girls would look up to them and want to follow in their footsteps.

And what did they do?

Two of them got drunk, right after the ceremony of consecration too, or within a few days of it.

Where they found the drink, I do not know. Somebody in the camp may have had a wine press, but where did they get the grapes? Somebody may have had a whisky still, but where did they get the grain? Perhaps the liquor had been brought out of Egypt by one of the "mixed multitude," but one hardly likes to think it was smuggled through the Red Sea on the night of the great deliverance. All we know for certain is that there was alcohol of some kind in the camp, and Nadab and Abihu drank of it.

They should have known better. Of all the people they should never have done any such thing. For anyone else it would have been a serious mistake, but for them, who had been set apart as ministers of God, it was a terrible sin.

It could have been that these two boys did not care very much about being chosen to work in the sanctuary. Perhaps they didn't want to be priests at all. Maybe they went through all the long consecration ceremony just because their father and uncle told them to. Certainly the washing Moses gave

10

them did not cleanse their hearts, nor did the blood on their toes keep them from walking to a place where drink was sold.

But the sin of drinking was as nothing to the crime that the drink made them commit.

Under the influence of liquor they made fun of their sacred duties. Jokingly they asked each other why they had to light their censers at the golden altar of incense in the tabernacle. Why couldn't they light them any way they pleased? What difference would it make if they put fire in their censers themselves?

So "Nadab and Abihu, the sons of Aaron, took either of them his censer, and put fire therein, and put incense thereon, and offered strange fire before the Lord, which he commanded them not."

The two boys may even have walked unsteadily through the tabernacle, swinging their censers irreverently, with no thought of the sacred meaning of what they were supposed to be doing. We shall never know exactly what they did, but God was very displeased with them. Not only had they disobeyed Him, but they had made light of holy, sacred things. Though He had trusted and honored them above all the young people in the camp, they had failed Him.

For such a deed they had to be punished. God could not let disobedience and insolence of this sort go by unrebuked.

And so it happened that, as Nadab and Abihu were staggering around the tabernacle with "strange fire" in their censers, there came a flash of light from the mercy seat, where now no mercy was possible, and the poor, foolish boys were suddenly burned to death. "And there went out fire from the Lord, and devoured them, and they died before the Lord."

The shocking news soon spread through the camp. People were stunned to think that two of those who had just been consecrated to the priesthood should so soon have proved unfaithful.

Because they were Aaron's sons, everybody expected there would be a big funeral. But there was none. Moses would not allow it. Instead, he told two old men to carry the bodies out of the camp and bury them. There was to be no mourning for two such naughty boys. Even Aaron was told he must not weep for them.

It must have seemed very hard to Aaron. Not only had he lost two of his sons, but he wasn't allowed to cry over them, as any father would want to do.

Then it was that the Lord spoke to him and said, "Do not drink wine nor strong drink, thou, nor thy sons with thee, when ye go into the tabernacle of the congregation, lest ye die: it shall be a statute for ever throughout your generations: and that ye may put difference between holy and unholy, and between unclean and clean."

Now Aaron understood. Drink had robbed him of his sons. Drink had confused their brains so they couldn't see any difference between the holy and the unholy. Drink had led them into this awful folly, and brought upon them the swift judgment of God.

STORY 2

God and the Grumblers

NOT long after the death of Nadab and Abihu somebody noticed that the cloud that had hovered over the tabernacle for the past seven weeks seemed to be moving again.

Word spread like wildfire through the camp.

"The cloud! Look at the cloud! It's moving."

It was. And it was moving toward the Promised Land.

What excitement! They were going to leave Sinai at last! In a little while they would be in Canaan! It seemed too good to be true.

Eagerly the people packed up their goods and folded their tents ready for the journey. Cattle and sheep were rounded up. Oxen were harnessed to the wagons.

The Levites began to take the tabernacle apart, and roll up the massive curtains, covering the precious furniture with cloths that had been made for this purpose.

Soon the whole camp was on the march.

For three days they journeyed. Once more the cloud stood still, the Levites put up the tabernacle, and the twelve tribes camped around it. At first the people were very happy —happier indeed than they had been since that wonderful night when they left Egypt. They felt that they were on their way at last. Soon they would be in Canaan, land of their dreams.

So they thought. But it was not to be. They were not ready for Canaan. They had many lessons still to learn. They had seen God's miracle at the Red Sea. They had heard His voice from Mount Sinai. They had eaten His manna every day for many months. But they did not truly love Him. Their faith in Him was still very weak.

They had not been at their new campsite many days when grumbling broke out again. Some complained about one thing, and some about another. Some didn't like the fearful desert they were in, and wished they were back at Sinai. Others said there wasn't enough grass for their cattle. Others thought they had to walk too far to get water. "And when the people complained it displeased the Lord."

Fire broke out in the camp. Many people were burned to death. When the people cried to Moses for help, he prayed to God, and "the fire was quenched."

But even this lesson did not stop the grumbling for long. Soon it began again. Some of the "mixed multitude" who had come along with Israel from Egypt began it this time, but the Israelites were quick to join them. Now the trouble was food. They were tired of the manna and wanted meat.

"Who shall give us flesh to eat?" they cried. "We remember the fish, which we did eat in Egypt freely; the cucumbers, and the melons, and the leeks, and the onions, and the garlick: but now our soul is dried away: there is nothing at all, beside this manna."

There was a sneer in their voices as they said "this manna," and God did not like it. And He liked it less when they all began to weep about it, "every man in the door of his tent."

Poor, foolish people! They could remember all the good things they had had to eat in Egypt, but had forgotten the bondage they had endured, the taskmasters, the beatings, and the heavy work. Yes, and they had forgotten all that God had done for them during their fourteen months of freedom.

Once more Moses turned to God for help. "Whence should I have flesh to give unto all this people?" he said, "for they weep unto me, saying, Give us flesh, that we may eat."

God told him not to worry. He would see that the people got flesh, and that it would last them a whole month.

"But how?" asked Moses. "The people, among whom I am, are six hundred thousand footmen; and thou hast said, I will give them flesh, that they may eat a whole month. Shall the flocks and the herds be slain for them . . . ? or shall all the fish of the sea be gathered together for them?"

"And the Lord said unto Moses, Is the Lord's hand waxed short? thou shalt see now whether my word shall come to pass unto thee or not."

15

Moses should have remembered, too, for the Lord had helped him out of a tight corner like this once before, soon after the Israelites had left Egypt.

Next day the wind began to blow from the Red Sea, and with it came the quails again, only this time in countless thousands. The air was thick with them. They flew in very low—about three feet above the ground—and as they did so the people knocked them down with sticks or caught them with their bare hands. Every man and woman, every boy and girl, collected heaps of them.

What a feast! They had cried for flesh; now they had it, all they could eat. For days and days they ate nothing but quail, morning, noon, and night. They didn't bother about the manna, just the quail. And they ate quail flesh until they were sick of the very sight of it.

Many ate so much they became ill. A plague broke out. Hundreds died of food poisoning and overeating. Every day there were more and more funerals.

So many people died that this first stopping place on the road to Canaan was given a new name: Kibroth-hattaavah. It's a long name, but it's worth remembering. It means "the graves of lust." That's where the greedy people were buried.

STORY 3

Two Missing Men

THE endless grumbling was almost too much for Moses. And no wonder. It was a hard enough job trying to take a million men, women, and children through a hot, dry, barren wilderness without having to put up with all their faultfinding.

When Moses prayed about it God told him to choose seventy of the best men of Israel and form a council to take a good share of his load. Then he wouldn't get all the blame when things seemed to go wrong.

Jethro, his father-in-law, had once told him the same thing, and at that time Moses had appointed rulers over thousands, hundreds, fifties, and tens. But even so he was still killing himself with work and worry.

"Gather unto me seventy men of the elders of Israel," God said, "whom thou knowest to be the elders of the people, and officers over them; and bring them unto the tabernacle of the congregation, that they may stand there with thee."

Obediently Moses made out a list of the best men he knew in the camp. Then he sent word to them to meet him at the door of the tabernacle.

Strangely, only sixty-eight came. When the roll was called, two were missing—Eldad and Medad. Their names suggest that they may have been brothers, maybe twins.

Why they did not come when Moses called them the Bible does not say. Certainly it couldn't have been because they were rebellious, or obstinate, or anything of the sort. If they *had* been, Moses would never have chosen them to be members of the new council of Israel. Possibly they were doing some kind deed for somebody, and couldn't leave it, or they didn't feel worthy of the honor that Moses had offered them.

Anyway, they didn't come, and Moses had to go on without them. He set the sixty-eight leaders "round about the tabernacle" and waited for God to act.

Suddenly the pillar of cloud came down very close to them all—so near that they could hear God speak to Moses. Then something very wonderful happened. The Spirit of God came upon them all, and "they prophesied, and did not cease."

TWO MISSING MEN

It must have been like what happened about fifteen hundred years later at Pentecost, when the Holy Spirit came upon the disciples and they began to talk about the wonderful things of God.

Now we can see why Moses placed the sixty-eight men "round about the tabernacle." If they had been bunched together, and had all begun talking at once, there would have been great confusion; but now each man had his own audience. And as the people who had gathered around the tabernacle listened to the beautiful things the men were saying, they were impressed that Moses had chosen true men of God to be their spiritual leaders.

In the midst of all the excitement a young man pressed through the crowd and came running to Moses, crying, "Eldad and Medad do prophesy in the camp."

So God had not forgotten the two missing men, even though they hadn't felt able, for some reason or other, to come to the meeting at the tabernacle. He had put His Spirit upon them too, which proves that they must both have been very good men.

But Joshua didn't like what was going on.

"My lord Moses," he cried, "forbid them."

He was afraid lest, if other people began prophesying in the camp, it would take away some of Moses' power and authority. But Moses didn't mind.

"Enviest thou for my sake?" he said, "would God that all the Lord's people were prophets, and that the Lord would put his spirit upon them!"

Moses wasn't a bit jealous because other people were beginning to do the things that he had been trying to do all by himself up to now. He was ready to share the glory of leadership, if this was God's will. Why should he worry if Eldad and Medad were prophesying in the camp? There would be seventy people doing this from now on, and he wished everybody in Israel were worthy of the honor.

Those words of Moses, "Would God that all the Lord's people were prophets," are among the finest in the Bible. We should all try to remember them. For willingness to share the joys and rewards of leadership is a sign of real nobility. Only little, selfish people try to keep the best things, the first places, the highest honors, all to themselves.

STORY 4

Trouble in the Family

IT IS sometimes said that "it never rains but it pours." Certainly Moses must have thought so when, right after the people had grumbled about their food, he found that his own brother and sister were talking against him.

This must have been very hard to take, for he loved Aaron and Miriam very much. Was not Miriam the big sister who had watched over him when, as a baby, he had been put in the ark among the bulrushes on the bank of the river Nile? Had not Aaron once walked all the way from Egypt to Mount Sinai to see him? Had not all three of them worked and worried and prayed together over the great task of bringing Israel out of Egypt?

What could be the matter with them? They were behaving like two naughty children, instead of two elderly grownups, as they were.

First they began to tease Moses about his wife. Because she was a Midianite and dark complexioned, they said she was an Ethiopian, or a Cushite. No doubt they had said this in fun many times before, but now there was a cruel barb in it that Moses didn't like.

Next they said, "Hath the Lord indeed spoken only by Moses? hath he not spoken also by us?"

Ah! So this was it! They were jealous about something.

Moses wondered what it could be. Did they want his job? Were they tired of his being in charge?

Then he remembered. Of course! Like Joshua, they were unhappy about the appointment of the seventy elders and the fact that God's Spirit had been poured out upon them. They were afraid they wouldn't be quite so important in the camp from now on. Moses, they thought, should have consulted them before doing anything like this.

Dear, dear! This was terrible! If Aaron and Miriam were beginning to grumble like the others, then things had got to a pretty bad place. What could be done about it?

There was nothing that Moses could do. In naming the seventy elders he had only done as God had told him; and as for their receiving the Holy Spirit, surely he had not been responsible for that. And he was not one to argue for himself. Indeed, the Bible says that by this time he had become the meekest man "upon the face of the earth."

Here was a situation where God had to step in. And He would have to settle the matter in a big way to make sure there would be no further misunderstanding. So, while the three were talking together rather heatedly, maybe in Moses' tent, "the Lord spake suddenly unto Moses, and unto Aaron,

22

and unto Miriam, Come out ye three unto the tabernacle of the congregation."

This was an order.

They went, no doubt wondering what was going to happen next.

Arriving at the tabernacle, they saw the pillar of cloud come down very low, until all three of them seemed to be shut in, as it were, with God.

Then God spoke.

"Aaron and Miriam," He said, and the two stepped forward.

"Hear now my words," said the Lord. "If there be a prophet among you, I the Lord will make myself known unto him in a vision, and will speak unto him in a dream." But, He went on, "my servant Moses is not so, who is faithful in all mine house. With him will I speak mouth to mouth, even apparently [clearly], and not in dark speeches; and the

similitude of the Lord shall he behold: wherefore then were ye not afraid to speak against my servant Moses?"

Aaron and Miriam stood silent and afraid, for it was clear that God was very displeased with them for what they had said to their brother. They waited to see whether God would speak again, but He didn't. Then the cloud rose, and the three found themselves standing together under the brilliant desert sunshine.

Suddenly Miriam let out a scream.

"Look at me!" she cried. "Look! I've got the leprosy!"

"And Aaron looked upon Miriam, and, behold, she was leprous."

This was a terrible thing to happen to anyone, for in those days leprosy was looked upon as an incurable disease. It gradually ate away a person's fingers and toes, and it was so contagious that anyone who got it had to be put out of the camp at once.

It was a most touching moment. Miriam, all broken up, was weeping her heart out at her awful punishment. Aaron,

24

sick with worry and very repentant, was pleading for forgiveness for himself and his sister. And Moses, whom Miriam had hurt most of all by her bitter tongue, was on his knees imploring God to heal her.

Never, perhaps, in all history, was there such a pathetic family scene.

And God was watching it all. His heart of love was deeply moved. He heard Moses' prayer. Miriam was healed. But just so she wouldn't forget her lesson, He ordered that she be put out of the camp for seven days. Then she could return, and all would be well again.

So poor Miriam was led to the edge of the camp and put outside, like anyone else who had had the leprosy. No doubt Moses and Aaron went along to comfort her and bid her good-by. And I am sure they were at the selfsame spot a week later to welcome her back with open arms.

STORY 5

So Near and Yet So Far

≈≈≈≈≈≈≈≈≈≈≈≈≈≈≈≈≈≈≈≈≈≈≈≈

DO YOU know how far it is from Mount Sinai to the border of Canaan? Less than 150 miles! If there had been a good modern road across the desert in those days—which there wasn't—and if Israel had owned a few hundred trucks—which they didn't—they could have covered the whole distance in four or five hours.

Even as things were—moving only as fast as the littlest lamb, or the youngest child, or the most obstinate donkey— the caravan was only eleven traveling days making the journey.

So it couldn't have been very long after all the trouble over the quail, and the worse trouble between Moses, Aaron, and Miriam, that they drew near to the land of their dreams.

Here at last, just about fifteen months after their great deliverance from Egypt, they caught their first glimpse of the green hills and fertile valleys of their future home.

What excitement there must have been in the camp! I can imagine mothers hugging their children for joy at the very thought that the hard, trying days in the wilderness, with all the heat, the thirst, and the weariness, would soon be over. Boys and girls shouted for joy as they pictured the land flowing "with milk and honey" they had heard their fathers talk about. Fancy! All the milk they could drink! All the honey they could eat! What a land it must be!

Then the people were told to rest in camp while twelve men, one from each tribe, went ahead to explore the country and find out what would have to be done to get possession of it.

These men, every one a ruler, were to spread out all over the place and learn how many people lived there, how strongly their cities were fortified, what sort of food they were growing, and whether there were any trees for lumber.

It was a great honor to be chosen for this mission. Each tribe sent its best man. All were "heads of the children of Israel." Much depended upon them—more than they knew!

Caleb was sent by the tribe of Judah, and Joshua by the tribe of Ephraim. There were ten others, whose names nobody remembers today.

27

SO NEAR AND YET SO FAR

As the twelve set forth there were many good-bys and good wishes from the thousands who gathered to see them off. Then, when the last had disappeared from view, the rest went back to their tents to await the spies' return.

A week passed, two weeks, three weeks. Still there was no word. What could have happened? Could all twelve have been slain by the Canaanites?

Four weeks, five weeks—how long the waiting time seemed! Then on the fortieth day they came back.

All were loaded down with various kinds of fruit. And how good it must have seemed to people who had lived in a wilderness so long! But the object that caught everybody's eye was a huge bunch of grapes—so large that it took two men to carry it. If this was the produce of Canaan, what a wonderful place it must be!

As for the spies, they said they had never seen such a country. "We came unto the land whither thou sentest us, and surely it floweth with milk and honey; and this is the fruit of it."

Up to this moment everybody had been happy. Faces were wreathed in smiles. Everybody wanted to go to Canaan at once. Then came the bad news.

"Nevertheless the people be strong that dwell in the land, and the cities are walled, and very great: and moreover we saw the children of Anak there."

As some of the spies continued to describe how strong the people of Canaan were, and how difficult it would be to take the land away from them, the hearts of the Israelites

29

←— PAINTING BY FRANK FORD   © 1954, BY REVIEW AND HERALD

The twelve spies sent to spy out the land of Canaan came back after a long time with wonderful samples of the fruit they had found there. The people rejoiced at their story.

sank. It was an awful blow to them. They had thought everything was going to be easy, just like the falling of the manna
and the quails being blown in by the wind. But this—this
was terrible.

Once more they began to murmur and complain.

But Caleb "stilled the people before Moses, and said, Let
us go up at once, and possess it; for we are well able to
overcome it."

It was a brave thing to say at such a time, for all the rest
—almost all—were against him. Ten of the men who went
with him cried out, "We be not able to go up against the
people; for they are stronger than we."

It was two against ten—for Joshua stood with Caleb—
and the people took the word of the ten. Their hopes were
dashed, and they gave way to despair. "And all the congregation lifted up their voice, and cried; and the people wept
that night."

Next morning they were all in an ugly mood, seething

30

with hatred of Moses and God, and full of open rebellion.

"Would God that we had died in the land of Egypt!" they cried; and, "Would God we had died in this wilderness!" Then someone raised the cry, "Let us make a captain, and let us return into Egypt."

The disappointment was almost more than they could bear. But at that moment Caleb and Joshua stood before the raging throng and cried, "The land, which we passed through to search it, is an exceeding good land. If the Lord delight in us, then he will bring us into this land, and give it us."

"Stone them! Stone them!" cried the people.

But there were no stones thrown. Suddenly the glory of the Lord appeared in the tabernacle, and the angry crowd was hushed. Israel waited, ashamed and afraid, to hear what God would say.

They had not long to wait. But when God spoke, they saw what an awful mistake they had made.

They had said they wished they had died in the wilderness. All right, said God, they should have their wish. "All those men which have seen my glory, and my miracles, which I did in Egypt and in the wilderness, and have tempted me now these ten times, and have not hearkened to my voice; surely they shall not see the land which I sware unto their fathers." "In this wilderness they shall be consumed, and there they shall die."

Back to the wilderness! Shut out of Canaan forever! The heartbreak of it! What a terrible price to pay for failing to trust God!

STORY 6

The Great Rebellion

YOU can imagine how the people felt; and the dawn of another day found them hopelessly discouraged. I can almost hear the children asking their mothers, "Aren't we going to get the milk and honey today?"

"No, darlings, not today," the heartbroken mothers replied, "not for many, many days."

Then the children cried too.

Some of the men climbed a mountain peak to look again at the land they had hoped for and dreamed about so long. From here it seemed so near that they thought it was a shame to leave it and go back into the wilderness.

"Lo, we be here," they said to one another, "and will go up unto the place which the Lord hath promised."

But it was too late.

When Moses heard about their plan he sent word to them not to try it. "Go not up, for the Lord is not among you," he said; "that ye be not smitten before your enemies.

THE GREAT REBELLION

For the Amalekites and the Canaanites are there before you, and ye shall fall by the sword: because ye are turned away from the Lord, therefore the Lord will not be with you."

But they went just the same, and no good came of it. Singing and shouting to keep up their courage, they marched across the border. But they never captured even the first hill. The people who lived there came and drove them out.

It was a very sorry group of men who returned to the camp that night. They knew now that it was no use trying to go into Canaan. Their last hope had gone.

Soon almost the whole camp was talking angrily against Moses. Why should they have to listen to that old man? What a mess he had made of everything! Had he not taken fifteen months for a journey that should have been over in two weeks? And now that they had reached the border of Canaan at last, he wanted them to go back into the dreadful wilderness for another forty years. Absurd! They wouldn't do it. Why should they? Who was Moses anyway?

The great rebellion was on.

The leader was Korah, a cousin of Moses and about the same age. He may even have looked like Moses, for both had the same grandfather—Kohath, the son of Levi. Perhaps this was one reason why so many others were ready to follow him. Anyway, he stirred up no less than "two hundred and fifty princes of the assembly, famous in the congregation, men of renown," and together they marched on Moses and Aaron.

"You take too much upon yourselves," they said insolently. "If all the congregation is holy, and the Lord is among them, why do you set yourselves above them?"

"*You* take too much upon yourselves," replied Moses, using their own words. Then he told them he was willing to let the Lord decide who should be the leader.

"Take you censers," he told them; "and put fire therein, and put incense in them before the Lord to morrow: and it shall be that the man whom the Lord doth choose, he shall be holy."

Then he sent messengers to fetch the other two conspirators, Dathan and Abiram, members of the tribe of Reuben. But they refused to come. Instead they sent back this impudent message: "Is it a small thing that thou hast brought us up out of a land that floweth with milk and honey, to kill us in the wilderness? . . . Thou hast not brought us into a land that floweth with milk and honey, or given us inheritance of fields and vineyards: wilt thou put out the eyes of these men? we will not come up."

34

THE GREAT REBELLION

No one had ever talked to Moses like this before, and he was very angry. To think that they spoke of Egypt as a land flowing with milk and honey—Egypt, the land of their bondage! And to think they would suggest he wanted to be a dictator who would put out the eyes of those who disagreed with him!

"Lord!" he cried in his sorrow, "I have not taken one ass from them, neither have I hurt one of them."

The time of test had come. God's whole plan of salvation was in danger. If the rebels should win, all He had tried to do for Israel would be lost.

That night the whole camp was filled with excited rumors. In hundreds of tents bitter, angry words were spoken. Friends of Korah, Dathan, and Abiram went everywhere urging everybody to meet at the tabernacle in the morning to see the end of Moses and his tyranny.

Early next morning, as the people were coming toward the tabernacle, God said to Moses and Aaron, "Separate yourselves from among this congregation, that I may consume them in a moment. And they fell upon their faces, and said, O God, the God of the spirits of all flesh, shall one man sin, and wilt thou be wroth with all the congregation?"

So in this moment of crisis these two dear old men prayed for the very people who were plotting against them!

Then Moses strode through the gathering crowd to the tent where Korah, Dathan, and Abiram were meeting.

"Stand back, stand back!" he called to the seething throng of onlookers. "Depart, I pray you, from the tents of these wicked men, . . . lest ye be consumed in all their sins."

A great silence fell as he spoke again. "Hereby ye shall know that the Lord hath sent me to do all these works," he said; "for I have not done them of mine own hand. If these men die the common death of all men, . . . then the Lord hath not sent me. But if the Lord make a new thing, and the earth open her mouth, and swallow them up, . . . and they go down quick into the pit; then ye shall understand that these men have provoked the Lord."

"Now he has surely gone too far!" some said. "Does he think he can make the earth open to swallow his enemies?"

Hardly had they spoken than there was a terrible roar and the earth did open—right where Korah, Dathan, and Abiram were standing. Suddenly all three of them, with all they owned, "went down alive into the pit, and the earth closed upon them."

Shrieks filled the air as the people fled in panic. Then sheets of flame swept about the 250 men with the fire-filled censers, and all were burned to death.

You would think that this would have been enough to convince everybody as to who was right and who was wrong, but no.

36

THE GREAT REBELLION

"You have killed the people of the Lord!" shouted the friends of the rebels. As they did so people began to fall down, right and left, all through the crowd.

Even Moses was surprised. "There is wrath gone out from the Lord," he cried to Aaron; "the plague is begun."

Afraid that perhaps, after all, God would consume everybody, he called to his brother, "Take a censer, and put fire therein from off the altar, and put on incense, and go quickly unto the congregation, and make an atonement for them."

Aaron went. With his smoking censer in his hand he "ran into the midst of the congregation."

Imagine it! The kindly old man, eighty-five years of age, running this way and that, waving his censer and crying to God to spare the people who had done so great a wrong!

Here was love most wonderful. The Bible says that Aaron "stood between the dead and the living; and the plague was stayed."

STORY 7

Flowers on a Stick

THE great rebellion was over. Nearly 15,000 people had died in the plague, besides the 250 leaders who had been burned by the fire, and the families of Korah, Dathan, and Abiram who had disappeared when the earth opened and swallowed them up. The rest were badly frightened, and thankful to be alive.

The trouble had broken out because everybody was so disappointed at being told they could not go into Canaan for another forty years, but it had been brewing for a long time. It may well have been that from the moment Aaron was made high priest his cousin Korah had been jealous of him. By talking against Aaron to other Levites, he had thought he might someday get his job. So with Dathan and Abiram. They had been jealous of Moses because he was leader and they were not. So they too had stirred up strife till open rebellion broke out.

Now they were gone. But had those who were spared

FLOWERS ON A STICK

learned their lesson? Were they all agreed now that God wanted Moses and Aaron to lead them? It looked like it for the moment, but who could be quite sure? Because so many Levites had been severely punished, perhaps many were wondering whether God had rejected them as custodians of the tabernacle.

To help make His wishes plain, God told Moses to tell the leaders of the twelve tribes to come to the tabernacle. Each was to bring his rod with him—the long stick men carried in those days when they went walking.

The twelve men came as ordered. Aaron was with them, as head of the tribe of Levi. Being the most important men in the camp, they all must have wondered why Moses had sent for them. No doubt they suspected it might have something to do with the sad events of the past few days.

Imagine their surprise when Moses asked them to hand him their rods. Whatever could he want with them?

As each leader handed over his rod, Moses carefully wrote the man's name on it before placing it with the other rods.

This must have taken quite a time, and meanwhile the twelve men wondered and wondered what was going to happen next.

When all twelve names had been written on the twelve rods—so clearly that there could be no possible mistake—Moses gathered all the rods in his arms and carried them into the tabernacle. When he came out again he told the men they could go now, but they were to come back the next day. Then God would show them by a miracle which of the twelve tribes he had chosen to conduct the services of the sanctuary and which man was His chosen leader. The sign would be the blossoming of this man's rod. There would be buds and flowers on the dry old stick.

Rodless, but excited, the twelve returned to their tents. Perhaps, they thought, God was going to make a change in the leadership of Israel, and this was His way of telling them. Someone other than Aaron might be high priest tomorrow. Which of them would it be?

As they went on their way people must have noticed that they had no rods.

"Have you lost your rods?" they asked.

"Oh, no, we all left them at the tabernacle," they replied. "We are waiting to see which one of them will blossom and bear fruit."

Next morning there was quite a crowd at the tabernacle to learn the result. Which, if any, of the twelve rods had blossomed?

When the twelve leaders had arrived, Moses went into the tabernacle. Even he was surprised at what he saw. For

40

one of the rods had not only buds and blossoms on it but ripe almonds as well.

Then he brought the twelve rods outside. You can imagine how astonished everybody was when they saw that one of the rods had turned into a tree overnight.

"Whose rod is it?" they cried.

"Come and see," said Moses.

The twelve men pressed eagerly forward. Then they saw the name. It was quite clear and unmistakable, despite all the blossoms and the almonds around it.

"Aaron!" they said as one man.

So there was to be no change in leadership, after all. And they were all satisfied, for there could be no doubt that God had spoken. Clearly He still wanted the tribe of Levi to care for the tabernacle, and Aaron to be high priest.

Aaron, by the way, was the only man who didn't get his rod back, for God told Moses to take it into the tabernacle and keep it there "for a token against the rebels" and to "quite take away their murmurings."

And it did take away their murmurings for a while, but not for very long. All too soon they were grumbling again.

41

STORY 8

Water From a Rock

FOR the next forty years the children of Israel wandered in the wilderness. Little is known of what happened to them then. Slowly, wearily, they moved from place to place, staying just long enough for the cattle to eat what little grass they could find. Then on they went again, scorched by the blistering sun, with no purpose and no hope. It was enough to break their hearts. Many times they must have thought what an awful price they were paying for their lack of faith in God.

One by one all who had taken part in the great rebellion died. Before the forty years had passed, at least six hundred thousand graves dotted the cruel and lonely desert.

Great as was their suffering, however, God did not utterly forsake them. Every day, except the seventh day of each week, He sent them manna to eat. Every day, from the moment Moses struck the rock in Horeb, soon after they came out of Egypt, there was water for them to drink. Not that it flowed all the way from Horeb, but always, just when most needed, it came bubbling up out of the rocky soil.

The prophet Isaiah wrote long afterward, "They thirsted not when he led them through the deserts; he caused the waters to flow out of the rock for them; he clave the rock also, and the waters gushed out." David recalled that the water "ran in dry places like a river."

Then one day, as their wanderings were coming to an end, the flow of water ceased. Having carefully counted the years of their punishment, they should have taken this as a sign that Canaan was again very near. But they didn't. Instead, once more they came grumbling to Moses and Aaron— now two very old men.

"Would God that we had died when our brethren died before the Lord!" they wailed. "And why have ye brought up the congregation of the Lord into this wilderness, that we

and our cattle should die there? And wherefore have ye made us to come up out of Egypt, to bring us into this evil place? it is no place of seed, or of figs, or of vines, or of pomegranates; neither is there any water to drink."

It was the same old story, the same old complaint. Just as soon as things began to go wrong, they wished they were back in Egypt, and were ready to blame Moses for all their troubles.

Just as they had done so many times before, Moses and Aaron turned to God for help. Going to the door of the tabernacle, they fell upon their faces. "And the glory of the Lord appeared unto them." They might be old and weary, but God was still the same as ever, still ready to show them the way out of their problems.

"Gather thou the assembly," He told them, "and speak ye unto the rock before their eyes; . . . and thou shalt bring forth to them water out of the rock."

So Moses and Aaron called all the people to come to the great rock that towered above the camp. Standing beneath it, Moses cried, "Hear now, ye rebels; must *we* fetch you water out of this rock?"

That is where he made a great mistake. He let himself get angry, which no leader should do; and this caused him to forget to give God the glory for the miracle, which was mistake number two. Then he made his third mistake, the worst of all, when he "lifted up his hand, and with his rod he smote the rock twice."

The water gushed forth; the people, overjoyed, stooped

mpatient at the rebellion of the children of srael, Moses struck the rock twice instead of speaking to it as he had been commanded, et God in His mercy sent streams of water.

down to drink; the cattle, parched with thirst, came running toward the cool, sparkling stream; but Moses and Aaron stood alone—in disgrace.

"Because ye believed me not," God said to them, "to sanctify me in the eyes of the children of Israel, therefore ye shall not bring this congregation into the land which I have given them."

The hearts of the two old men sank. Not go into Canaan? After all that they had done for Israel, all the trials they had endured, all the long, long journey they had traveled? Surely God did not mean that! How could He? What had they done to deserve so great a punishment?

What had they done?

Because they had not obeyed God *exactly,* they had spoiled something very beautiful. They had ruined a most important lesson that He wanted to teach not only to Israel but to people in all the world.

The rock was a type of Christ. He was to be struck once, but never again. He was to be *"once* offered to bear the sins of many," not many times, over and over again.

Moses had struck the rock once—at Horeb. That was right. He had been told to do that. But now he had struck it again, twice, in fact. And God had told him to *speak* to it— not to strike it—just as sinners may speak to Christ anywhere, in every time of need, and bring the water of life into their souls.

Poor Moses and Aaron! Maybe they didn't understand all this as we do now. But God did not blame them for failing to understand but for failing to believe and obey.

STORY 9

A Sad Farewell

THE news that he would not be allowed to enter Canaan was enough to make Moses give up everything then and there. He was terribly disappointed. Who wouldn't have been? But give up? Never! As long as he had life and health he would lead Israel toward the Promised Land.

Forgetting himself, he began to plan the next step of the journey. He had made up his mind that the easiest way to get to Canaan was through the land of Edom, so he sent messengers to the king of that country, asking permission for Israel to pass through.

It was a very kind and friendly message, because the Edomites were also children of Abraham, through Ishmael. After telling the king about some of the hardships through which Israel had passed, Moses wrote, "Let us pass, I pray thee, through thy country: we will not pass through the fields, or through the vineyards, neither will we drink of the water of the wells: we will go by the king's high way, we will not turn to the right hand nor to the left, until we have passed thy borders."

But the king of Edom said No. "Thou shalt not pass by me," he replied, "lest I come out against thee with the sword."

It was a surly, selfish answer, but Moses refused to get angry about it. Instead, he sent another gracious note, assuring the king that Israel would keep to the highway and pay for any water that they might drink on their way through.

But still the king of Edom refused, and there was nothing to do but seek some other way to get to Canaan.

Moving on east and south to get around Edom, they came to Mount Hor, and here it was that a very sad thing happened. As the people pitched camp God told Moses that Aaron was going to die, and that He wanted both of them to go up to the top of the mountain and take Eleazar, Aaron's son, with them.

The three men started out, with Moses going ahead, then Aaron, and behind them Eleazar.

It must have been a very sad little procession that wended its way slowly—so very slowly—up the mountainside. For Aaron was 123 years old, and Moses only three years younger. They had been friends such a long, long time and had stood together through all sorts of troubles. Now they were to be parted.

I suppose they stopped many times on the way, just so they could talk a little longer and make the final walk together last as long as possible.

But little by little, step by weary step, they came near the top. Looking down, they saw the camp of Israel spread out on the plain below. Perhaps they told each other how much those poor, dear people meant to them, and how they had tried so hard to help them.

A few more steps brought them, panting, to the summit. Then something very touching took place. One by one Moses removed Aaron's priestly garments, placing them in turn upon Eleazar, as tears flowed down all their cheeks.

Then came the sad farewell.

"Good-by, son; God bless you."

"Good-by, Father."

Then the two brothers looked into each other's eyes for the last time.

"Farewell!" they said. And Aaron breathed his last, his brother's arms around him.

Down in the camp, far below, the people began to get worried. Why were Moses, Aaron, and Eleazar staying up on the mountain so long?

Then, looking up, they saw two figures coming down the winding path. Aaron was not with them, and his son was wearing his robes.

Quickly they guessed what had happened, and the sad message swept through the camp—"Aaron is dead!"

Though some had not liked him, and some had quarreled with him, now they all were sorry he was gone. And "they mourned for Aaron thirty days, even all the house of Israel."

PART II

Stories of the Conquest of Canaan

(Numbers 21:1-Joshua 24:33)

STORY 1

Serpent on a Pole

A MONTH after the death of Aaron, Moses ordered the children of Israel to strike camp and move on once more toward the Promised Land.

He knew there wasn't much time left now. The forty years of wandering in the wilderness were almost over.

Many in the camp besides Moses had been counting those years. Since the great rebellion of Korah, Dathan, and Abiram thousands of boys had grown to manhood, and girls to womanhood, in that hot, dry, desolate land in which they had been forced to live. They had married and had children of their own, waiting for the years to pass and longing for the day when they would be allowed to enter Canaan.

How slowly the years had passed! Ten, twenty, thirty years—each one marked by more and more funerals as the old folks who had come out of Egypt passed away. It must have seemed that the forty years of wilderness wandering would never end.

52

SERPENT ON A POLE

Thirty-five, thirty-six, thirty-seven, thirty-eight. At last the time was drawing near. Only two more years!

But now came a grievous disappointment. As the long caravan began to move onward again, the people noticed that instead of going due north they were traveling southeast, "by way of the Red sea, to compass the land of Edom."

This was too much. They didn't want to see the Red Sea any more. They wanted to go to Canaan by the shortest and quickest way possible. The thought of having to backtrack again almost broke their hearts. The Bible says that they were "much discouraged because of the way." It seemed to them as though they might be going to miss the Promised Land after all.

Grumbling broke out once more, and "the people spake against God, and against Moses," saying, "Wherefore have ye brought us out of Egypt to die in the wilderness? for there is no bread, neither is there any water; and our soul loatheth this light bread."

For a while it looked as if there might be another great rebellion, but suddenly something happened that changed everything. Poisonous serpents appeared all over the desert. Thou-

sands upon thousands of them. They crawled into the tents, the bedding, the wagons, the food supplies. They were all over the place. It was terrifying. Thousands of people were bitten and died.

Many tried to kill the serpents, but the more they killed, the more appeared. They couldn't eat or sleep for fear of them. There seemed no way to get rid of them.

At last the people came to Moses and begged for help. "We have sinned," they said, "for we have spoken against the Lord, and against thee; pray unto the Lord, that he will take away the serpents from us. And Moses prayed for the people."

Then it was that the Lord told Moses to do a very strange thing. He didn't tell him how to get rid of the serpents, but how to cure the people who had been bitten by them.

"Make thee a fiery serpent," God said, "and set it upon a pole: and it shall come to pass, that every one that is bitten, when he looketh upon it, shall live."

So Moses "made a serpent of brass, and put it upon a pole, and it came to pass, that if a serpent had bitten any man, when he beheld the serpent of brass, he lived."

A wonderful thing happened then. From every part of the camp came happy cries of, "I'm cured! I'm cured!" as dying people, looking at the brazen serpent, found themselves completely healed.

SERPENT ON A POLE

I can see a mother holding her little boy in her arms. She is desperately worried about him, for he is very ill. The poison is killing him. In a few more minutes he will be dead. She tries to get him to look at the brazen serpent on the pole.

"Look, darling, look!" she cries frantically.

"Look at what?" the poor boy asks weakly.

"The serpent, the brazen serpent! Only look, and you shall live!"

Slowly the boy turns his head. A smile spreads over his face. The pain has gone. He feels better at once.

All over the camp scenes like this were taking place as the children of Israel learned a lesson they needed very much: the power of faith in the word of God. For of course it wasn't

the brazen serpent that helped them. Not at all. A brazen serpent couldn't help anybody, any more than a brazen elephant or a brazen billy goat could. But when they did exactly as God told them, and *looked* at the serpent, their faith brought His power into their lives, and they were healed.

The children of Israel kept this brazen serpent for a long, long time. But as the years rolled by they forgot its true meaning and made an idol of it. They even burned incense to it as though it were a god. Centuries later good king Hezekiah destroyed it, calling it "Nehushtan," meaning "a piece of brass." And that's all it was, just a piece of brass that couldn't help or heal anybody.

Hundreds of years after that Jesus said to Nicodemus, "As Moses lifted up the serpent in the wilderness, even so must the Son of man be lifted up: that whosoever believeth in him should not perish, but have eternal life."

This is one of the most beautiful things Jesus ever said. He was "lifted up" on the cross of Calvary, and ever since then thousands of people in every land have looked to Him in faith and been saved from the curse of sin.

His promise still stands. It is for you and for me. It is for every boy and girl in the whole wide world.

Today, if you should be bitten by "that old serpent, which is called the Devil, and Satan," turn your eyes upon Jesus. Think about His cross. Remember His promise that *"whosoever"* believeth in Him shall not perish "but have eternal life." And the life of God will flow into your little life with all its healing, cleansing, forgiving power.

57

All who looked at the brazen serpent were healed from the bite of poisonous snakes. The story was to remind us of Jesus' power to save when we look to Him for help.

STORY 2

The Talking Donkey

FROM the moment that the children of Israel began to trust the word of God, as they did when they looked at the serpent on the pole, things began to go better for them.

Coming to the edge of the wilderness, they were made happy to see the more fertile land beyond. And here it was that Moses did something different from anything he had ever done before. He told the princes of Israel to dig a well with their rods, or staves!

Did you ever try to dig a hole in sand with a round stick? How far down did you get?

All the people gathered to watch the princes at work, and everybody was smiling. Just imagine how you would feel if you saw the elders of your church trying to dig a hole with long sticks! Of course they didn't get anywhere.

And then, wonder of wonders, water came bubbling up out of the very sand they had been trying in vain to move!

58

Thus God let them see once more that He was able and willing to provide for them, even when they could do but little for themselves.

At sight of the water the people began to sing, and their song ran like this, "Spring up, O well; sing ye unto it."

They were happy now. Here was new proof that God was with them. And from their faith came happiness, and from their happiness their first victories.

Moving northward, they asked Sihon, king of the Amorites, for permission to pass through his country, but he refused. Even though they promised not to go into his fields or his vineyards, but "go along by the king's high way," he came against them with all his soldiers. There was a big battle, and Israel won, sweeping on to take all his cities from the river Arnon up to the river Jabbok.

If you will look on the map on page 106, you will see that the river Arnon runs into the Dead Sea and the river Jabbok into the river Jordan. This will give you an idea how much land the children of Israel took from the Amorites and how they went up *east* of the Dead Sea to get to Canaan.

Og, king of Bashan, was the next to come against Israel. He was a giant, and his people lived in a rocky mountain fortress. But he too was defeated, and all his land taken from him.

By this time the rulers of other cities began to be afraid of Israel. One of these was Balak, king of the Moabites. He was so scared that he said to his friends the Midianites, "Now shall this company [meaning Israel] lick up all that are round about us, as the ox licketh up the grass of the field."

Then he got a bright idea. If he couldn't fight with Israel, perhaps he could get some sorcerer to curse them and so weaken them that he could drive them out of the land.

He thought of a man named Balaam who was supposed to be able to do this sort of thing. But Balaam lived in Mesopotamia, five hundred miles away. Was it worth sending so far?

Balak thought it was. His country was in deadly peril, and this seemed the only way out. So he sent messengers with a large sum of money to persuade Balaam to come.

"Behold," he said, "there is a people come out of Egypt: . . . they cover the face of the earth, and they abide over against me: come now therefore, I pray thee, curse me this people; for they are too mighty for me."

Balaam listened to what the messengers had to say, but refused to go with them. So they went all the way back to the land of Moab without him.

When Balak saw that Balaam hadn't come with his messengers, he was very upset. Then he chose some of the most important men in his country and sent them back to Balaam with more money than before, and with promises of great honors if only he would come and curse Israel.

This time Balaam decided to go. Saddling his ass, he "went with the princes of Moab."

THE TALKING DONKEY

It was no easy trip. Not only was it a very long journey and a very hot one, but, unknown to him, an angel had been sent from heaven to stop him from going to curse Israel.

As for that donkey he was riding—well, he never dreamed that it could see angels, and talk!

The first Balaam knew anything was wrong was when the donkey went right off the trail into a field. This annoyed him very much, for it made him look foolish in sight of his two servants and the princes of Moab. Of course, he didn't know that the donkey had seen an angel with a drawn sword in his hand, so he struck the poor animal and forced it back on the path.

Some distance farther on the donkey balked again. They were going along a narrow path through a vineyard. There was a wall on either side, and suddenly the donkey shied at something and crushed Balaam's foot against the wall. Again he was angry and struck the donkey a cruel blow.

By and by they came to a very narrow place, perhaps on the edge of a precipice, where there "was no way to turn either to the right hand or to the left." Here the donkey saw the angel again, and fell right down under Balaam. This made him more angry than ever, and he beat the donkey with a stick.

Now to his astonishment he heard a voice nobody ever heard before or since. The donkey was speaking! Of course it didn't speak English, but maybe Hebrew or Aramaic. What his voice sounded like nobody knows. But I'd like to have heard it, wouldn't you?

"What have I done unto thee," asked the donkey, "that thou hast smitten me these three times?"

"Because thou hast mocked me," said Balaam, angry that his animal had behaved so badly before such important people. "I would there were a sword in mine hand, for now would I kill thee."

"Am not I thine ass," said the poor little beast, "upon which thou hast ridden ever since I was thine unto this day? was I ever wont to do so unto thee?"

"Nay," agreed Balaam reluctantly.

"Then the Lord opened the eyes of Balaam," and he saw what the donkey had seen all along—the angel of the Lord "standing in the way, and his sword drawn in his hand."

Instantly Balaam fell flat on his face.

And what do you suppose the angel said to him first? He spoke about the poor little donkey, showing how God cares for animals.

"Wherefore hast thou smitten thine ass these three times?" he said. "I went out to withstand thee, because thy way is perverse before me: and the ass saw me, and turned from me these three times: unless she had turned from me, surely now also I had slain thee, and saved her alive."

"I have sinned," said Balaam, offering to go back home at once.

But the angel said, "Go with the men: but only the word that I shall speak unto thee, that thou shalt speak."

So Balaam went on with the princes to Moab.

Overjoyed at his arrival, King Balak took Balaam to a mountain peak where they could both look down on the camp of Israel.

"Now curse them for me," he said.

But Balaam couldn't do it. Instead, he blessed them.

Balak, annoyed, took him to another place, then another, but it was no use. Balaam couldn't think of a single curse to utter. He just said what the angel told him to say, and it was all blessing.

"Blessed is he that blesseth thee," he said of Israel, "and cursed is he that curseth thee."

This made Balak very angry, as well it might. "I called thee to curse mine enemies," he cried, thinking of all the money he had paid Balaam and of the princes he had sent to fetch him; "and, behold, thou hast altogether blessed them these three times. . . . Flee now to thy place."

Balaam fled—as fast as his little donkey would carry him.

I wonder what the donkey said to him on the way back? Wouldn't we all like to know!

STORY 3

Five Girls Make History

ISRAEL was now camped on the east of the river Jordan, right opposite the city of Jericho. Because it was nearly time for them to enter Canaan, and every able-bodied man would be needed for the invasion, God told Moses to count the people and find out just how many there were.

Forty years before, the number of men twenty years old and upward was 603,550. Now the count was 601,730.

This gives some idea of the awful number of deaths which took place in the wilderness. For all but two of the 603,550 died —all save Caleb and Joshua. Adding the wives of these men, and some of the children who died also, makes a total of over 1,200,000, and that's a lot of people to bury in so short a time.

While those in charge of the numbering were counting the men of the tribe of Manasseh, they got as far as Zelophehad, and stopped. For Zelophehad (a great-great-great-grandson of Joseph) was dead, and he had no sons, only daughters.

This meant that these girls, just because they were girls,

were left out of everything, as being of no importance. And they didn't like it. Not a bit! And did they make a fuss!

There must have been something very striking about these five girls, for they are mentioned by name several times in the Bible. Perhaps you should learn their names so you won't forget them. Here they are: Mahlah, Noah, Hoglah, Milcah, and Tirzah. I don't think I would choose any of these names for one of my daughters, but no doubt they were considered very pretty names back in those days. Be that as it may, these five girls really made history.

First of all, they asked to see Moses. He agreed to meet them and hear their story. Then they went to the tabernacle to keep the appointment, and what do you suppose? When they got there they found not only Moses waiting to greet them but Eleazar, the new high priest, and all the princes of the congregation, and almost everybody else in camp.

Bravely the five girls walked into the middle of that huge crowd, right up to the door of the tabernacle.

What courage they had! Girls had never dared to do anything like that before.

Just which one was the speaker I do not know. Perhaps it was Mahlah, the eldest; but it could have been Noah, or Hoglah, or Milcah, or Tirzah. One thing is sure, they didn't all try to speak at once as some girls I know would have done had they been there. They were too sensible for that.

Said one of them, "Our father died in the wilderness, and he was not in the company of them that gathered themselves

together against the Lord in the company of Korah; but died in his own sin, and had no sons. Why should the name of our father be done away from among his family, because he hath no son? Give unto us therefore a possession among the brethren of our father."

Moses listened patiently. It seemed to him that the girls' request was just. But before deciding, he said he would talk to God about it.

He did so, and God soon answered. He said to Moses, "The daughters of Zelophehad speak right: thou shalt surely give them a possession of an inheritance among their father's brethren; and thou shalt cause the inheritance of their father to pass unto them."

He added, "Thou shalt speak unto the children of Israel, saying, If a man die, and have no son, then ye shall cause his inheritance to pass unto his daughter."

So it was that these five girls made history. By standing for something they believed to be right, they became a blessing to all girls down the ages from that day to this. For the law of inheritance given by God at that time is very much the same as that in use in every civilized country today.

You will be glad to learn that all five girls got married. The Bible says so. "For Mahlah, Tirzah, and Hoglah, and Milcah, and Noah, the daughters of Zelophehad, were married unto their father's brothers' sons."

One almost feels that the story should finish, "And they lived happily ever after." Of course it doesn't, but I am sure they lived happily for a long, long time.

STORY 4

Lonely Journey

PLEASE, please, dear Lord, let me go over and see the land of Canaan," Moses prayed over and over again.

And no wonder! For eighty years he had dreamed about it. In the dark days in Egypt and all through the years of wandering in the wilderness, he had thought about it. When the people had become discouraged he had tried to cheer them up with stories of the good things they would enjoy in the Land of Promise.

Now he had arrived at the Jordan. Across it he could see Jericho and the mountains beyond. He was so near, and yet so far!

Again he cried to God, "I pray thee, let me go over, and see the goodly land that is beyond Jordan, that goodly mountain, and Lebanon."

But again God said No.

"Speak no more unto me of this matter," He said.

It must have been hard to take. And all because of that one sin when he had disobeyed God and struck the rock twice. Yet God's seeming hardness was really kindness in disguise. For Moses was now 120 years old, and God knew he wasn't strong enough to bear the burden of leading Israel through the days of battle ahead. It was better that younger hands should undertake the great new task.

"Get thee up into the top of Pisgah," God said to him, "and lift up thine eyes westward, and northward, and southward, and eastward, and behold it with thine eyes: for thou shalt not go over this Jordan. But charge Joshua, and encourage him, and strengthen him: for he shall go over before this people, and he shall cause them to inherit the land which thou shalt see."

Moses knew now that his end was near. The time had come for Israel to cross the Jordan, and he must be left behind. They would go on, and he would stay. Joshua would lead them, not he.

So he called the people together for the last time. They came flocking to him, as they had done so many times before.

Standing before the great congregation, he spoke in a voice as loud and clear as ever, for though he was old "his eye was not dim, nor his natural force abated." Hour after hour he retold the story of God's blessings through the forty years since the great deliverance from Egypt.

Most of those who listened had never seen Egypt. Many of them had been just boys and girls, or babes in their mothers' arms, at the crossing of the Red Sea. Many had only a faint memory of the giving of the law on Mount Sinai. As for the children, they knew nothing of these things except as their parents had told them.

So Moses began at the beginning and told the whole wonderful story over again, reminding them of the way God had sent them food and water and given them victory.

"All the way that ye went," he said, "the Lord thy God bare thee, as a man doth bear his son."

They all understood that, especially the smaller boys and girls. They remembered how their daddies picked them up when they were tired and put them on their shoulders.

God had been like a father to them all, helping them in every time of need. And why? Because He wanted them to be a good example to all other people in the world. He gave them the Ten Commandments, so that they would know the difference between right and wrong. He told them to build a sanctuary, so they would know that God expected them to be a pure and holy people.

"For thou art an holy people unto the Lord thy God," said Moses. "The Lord thy God hath chosen thee to be a special people unto himself, above all people that are upon the face of the earth."

Then he added, so they wouldn't have any wrong ideas, "The Lord did not set his love upon you, nor choose you, because ye were more in number than any people; for ye were the fewest of all people: but because the Lord loved you, and because he would keep the oath which he had sworn unto your fathers, hath the Lord brought you out with a mighty hand . . . from the hand of Pharaoh, king of Egypt."

Because God loved them so much there was nothing He would not do for them if only they would be true to Him.

"If thou shalt hearken diligently unto the voice of the Lord thy God, to observe and to do all his commandments," He said, "all these blessings shall come on thee, and overtake thee."

All sorts of blessings would come running after them, and catch up with them, and surprise them. They would be blessed in their cities and on their farms, at home and abroad, everywhere and in everything. "The Lord shall open unto thee his good treasure. . . . The Lord shall make thee the head, and not the tail."

So Moses tried to tell them how much good would come to them if they would keep close to God and remember to do His commandments.

But he also warned them of what would happen if they should forget God and turn away from Him. Instead of being

70

blessed, they would be cursed. Sickness, disease, and trouble of all kinds would come upon them. Instead of enjoying the Promised Land, they would be scattered among all nations.

"If thou wilt not observe to do all the words of this law that are written in this book," he said, "that thou mayest fear this glorious and fearful name, THE LORD THY GOD; then the Lord will make thy plagues wonderful." "And the Lord shall scatter thee among all people, from the one end of the earth even unto the other."

Closing his talk, he said, "See, I have set before thee this day life and good, and death and evil." "Therefore choose life."

Then Moses called Joshua before him and "in the sight of all Israel" he passed the leadership over to him. Bravely, but perhaps with tears in his eyes, he said to him, "Be strong and of a good courage: for thou must go with this people unto the land which the Lord hath sworn unto their fathers to give them. . . . And the Lord, he it is that doth go before thee; he will be with thee, he will not fail thee, nor forsake thee: fear not, neither be dismayed."

LONELY JOURNEY

Moses and Joshua then went together into the tabernacle "and the Lord appeared in the tabernacle in a pillar of a cloud." So the people knew that the choice of Joshua as their new leader was God's choice too.

Now the meeting is over. The people are streaming back to their tents. Some are weeping; others are talking about Joshua and the kind of leader he will make; the children are playing around as though nothing important had happened.

Silence settles upon the camp. Everybody turns in for the night—all save one.

Slowly through the darkening twilight moves the figure of a lonely old man. His work is done. His last command has been given. His last farewell has been said. Now he climbs Mount Nebo to "the top of Pisgah" to meet the One whom he has served so faithfully and so long.

There is no Aaron to go with him, no Eleazar, no Joshua, On his last sad journey he walks alone.

With the dawn he looks down upon the camp of the people he has loved so much. Then his eyes roam across the Jordan valley, westward, northward, southward. There it is! The beautiful land! The goodly land! For a moment it is all spread out before him in one glorious panorama. How wonderful! How well worth all the struggle, the toil, the waiting!

It is the last thing he sees on earth. Presently the old eyes close. He falls asleep in the arms of God.

"So Moses the servant of the Lord died there in the land of Moab. . . . And he buried him."

From the top of Pisgah, Moses took a long look at the fruitful valleys and grassy plains of the Promised Land, which Israel was now to inherit after their wilderness wanderings.

STORY 5

The Scarlet Cord

JOSHUA waited in the camp, wondering when Moses would return. But he did not come.

Perhaps he sent out search parties to look for him, but if so, they never found him. He just disappeared.

Then the Lord Himself broke the sad news, "Moses my servant is dead," and "the children of Israel wept for Moses thirty days." All were grieved to think that the grand old man would be with them no more. For a while there was a feeling of emptiness and loneliness in every heart.

Yet they could not mourn forever. There was work to be done. They must prepare for the great invasion.

To Joshua, God said, "Arise, go over this Jordan. . . . As I was with Moses, so I will be with thee: I will not fail thee, nor forsake thee. Be strong and of a good courage."

Joshua needed courage at this moment. The whole burden of leadership had just fallen on him. The task of planning for the future was now his, and his alone. No more could he go to Moses for advice. From now on he must make all the decisions himself.

He may well have been a bit worried as he thought of all he had to do, and this may be why God said to him again and again, "Be thou strong and very courageous."

The first thing he did on his own was to send two men across the Jordan to find out about the defenses of Jericho and learn anything else that might be of help in planning the attack.

These two spies got over the river all right and, mixing with the people going in and out of the city, managed to get inside without any trouble. Then, climbing to the top of the wall, they found some houses there and decided to rent a room for the night in one belonging to a woman named Rahab.

Thinking they were safe, they talked with Rahab and found out many things of interest. Suddenly, however, they heard the clank of arms below.

"The soldiers!" cried Rahab. "To the roof!"

The two spies fled upstairs as fast as they could go, Rahab following them. On the roof were stalks of flax, which Rahab quickly piled upon them. Then she hurried down to the door where the soldiers were already knocking loudly.

"In the king's name," they cried as she opened the door, "bring forth the men that are come to thee . . . : for they are come to search out all the country."

Rahab said she didn't know where the men came from or where they had gone. "Pursue after them quickly," she said; "for ye shall overtake them." Without searching the house the soldiers left hurriedly and hastened to the Jordan, feeling sure the spies must have gone that way.

Meanwhile, Rahab went back to the roof where, removing the stalks of flax, she talked to the two men again.

"I know that the Lord hath given you the land," she said, "and that . . . all the inhabitants of the land faint because of you. For we have heard how the Lord dried up the water of the Red sea for you, when ye came out of Egypt; and what ye did unto the two kings of the Amorites, that were on the other side of Jordan. . . . And as soon as we had heard these things, our hearts did melt."

THE SCARLET CORD

Rahab was sure the children of Israel would enjoy the same success when they crossed the Jordan, because their God "is God in heaven above, and in earth beneath." So she tried to make a bargain with the spies. She would help them to escape if they in turn would promise that she and all her relatives would be spared when Israel captured Jericho. They agreed.

So in the dead of night she let the men down over the wall with a scarlet cord. When they were ready to slip away into the darkness they whispered to her as loudly as they dared, "Bind this line of scarlet thread in the window." This was to tell the soldiers of Israel which house to spare.

As soon as the spies were gone Rahab pulled up the scarlet cord and tied it in the window of her house. And there it stayed for many days. Whenever Rahab looked at it, she told herself, "That will keep me safe." She was so sure of it that she persuaded her father and mother and all her brothers and sisters to come and stay in her house.

They believed her story. They came to trust in the scarlet cord. And how glad they were afterward! For when the city fell to the Israelites all in that house were saved.

It was just like when the Israelites sprinkled the blood of the lamb on the doorposts of their homes in Egypt, when the angel of death passed by. Every home with the blood was spared. So it will be in the future. Every heart that has the blood of Christ on its doorposts, or the scarlet cord of His love in the window, will be spared in the day of judgment.

77

← PAINTING BY FRED COLLINS

The two soldiers sent by Joshua to spy on Jericho found refuge in Rahab's home, and he helped them escape under cover of darkness on a red cord she hung from her window.

STORY 6

Crossing the Jordan

THE TWO spies hid in the mountains west of Jericho for three days. Then they made their way back across the Jordan to the camp of Israel.

Joshua was waiting for them. "The people are all afraid of us," they told him, recalling what Rahab had said.

Calling his officers, Joshua told them what the spies had found and that the hour for attack had come. Then he bade them go through the camp, and tell everyone to prepare food and be ready to move, for "within three days ye shall pass over this Jordan."

You can imagine the excitement as the people heard the news. The great moment for which they had waited so long had come at last! Only three days more, and they would be in Canaan. Next Sabbath they would spend in the land of milk and honey. It sounded too good to be true.

There was just one problem—the Jordan. Being in flood, it was almost a mile wide, including the swampland on either

78

side. How did Joshua plan to take a million people across it? Was he going to build a bridge, or boats—or what?

The three days went by quickly. Everybody was happy. Eagerly food was prepared, tents were folded, bedding was packed, wagons were loaded—but still there was no sign of any work being done on a bridge or a boat.

Word now went through the camp that everyone was to watch the Levites for the signal to start. "When ye see the ark of the covenant of the Lord your God, and the priests the Levites bearing it," said Joshua, "then ye shall remove from your place, and go after it."

All eyes now turned toward the center of the camp where the tabernacle had been standing for the past few weeks. It was no longer there. Already the gold-plated woodwork had been taken apart, the beautiful curtains carefully folded, and the articles of furniture reverently covered. Groups of Levites stood around awaiting an order from Joshua to pick up their precious burden and move on.

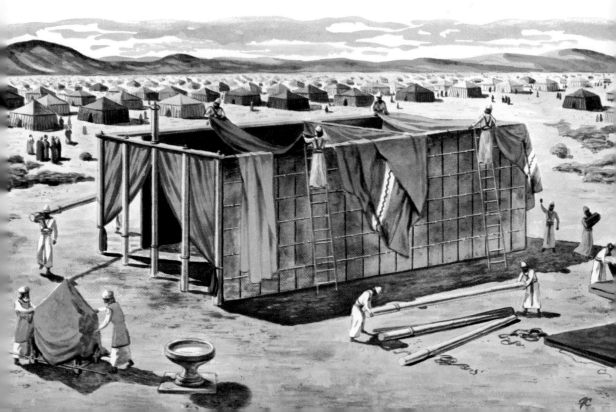

But still there was the Jordan, so wide and swift and deep. What *was* Joshua going to do about the Jordan? Then the day before the march was to begin he said to the people, "Sanctify yourselves: for to morrow the Lord will do wonders among you."

Now there was more excitement. The Lord had worked wonders for them before. What was He going to do now?

That last night was a night of prayer. Fathers and mothers, boys and girls, gave themselves anew to God and asked forgiveness for their sins. They wanted to be ready when He drew near.

Early next morning Joshua called the people together and said to them, "Come hither, and hear the words of the Lord your God. . . . Hereby ye shall know that the living God is among you. . . . Behold, the ark of the covenant of the Lord of all the earth passeth over before you into Jordan. . . . And it shall come to pass, as soon as the soles of the feet of the priests that bear the ark of the Lord, the Lord of all the earth, shall rest in the waters of Jordan, that the waters of Jordan shall be cut off from the waters that come down from above; and they shall stand upon an heap."

CROSSING THE JORDAN

A thrill sweeps through the waiting people. "Are we going to cross the Jordan on dry land as our fathers passed through the Red Sea?" they ask one another.

Now the priests bearing the ark are moving down the slope toward the river. Everyone holds his breath. Thousands of boys and girls stand on tiptoe to get a good view, wondering what is going to happen.

Nearer and nearer come the priests to the water's edge. Still the river rolls majestically by.

Nearer and nearer. Suppose nothing should happen? Will they just go on walking right into the water? Or will Joshua tell them to stop?

Nearer and nearer. Just a few steps more. Five, four, three, two, one.

Look! Their feet have touched the water!

Suddenly something happens. Nobody knows what. Only that the water is now ten feet away. Twenty feet. Thirty feet. A hundred feet. Now there seems to be dry land all the way across. To the right, to the left, there is no sign of water. Somehow, somewhere, miraculously, the river has been dammed up and has ceased to flow.

The priests move on. At Joshua's orders they stand still in the midst of the river bed, in the place of greatest danger should the water begin to flow again. Seeing them there, the people begin to cross. By thousands and tens of thousands they hurry from one side to the other, driving their wagons and their cattle as fast as they will go. It is an amazing sight.

The people of Jericho, watching from the walls of their city, are struck dumb with fear. They have never seen anything like this. Nor has anyone else.

Hour after hour the Israelites continue to cross until the last man, the last woman, the last little boy, and the last little girl are safely on the other side.

Now Joshua sends word to the priests holding the ark in the midst of the river bed to "come up out of Jordan."

They come, and are they glad! Hardly have they reached the bank when there is a dull roar somewhere in the distance and the pent-up waters come flooding all over the place where they had just been standing.

Everybody stares at the water in amazement. It is hard to believe. The river is in full flood as before! Yet a million people have crossed from one side to the other without bridge or boat! So this is the wonder God promised to perform!

82

To make sure the people would never forget this marvelous miracle, Joshua had told twelve men, one from each tribe, to carry twelve big rocks out of the midst of Jordan. Now he has them piled in a heap as a memorial of the great event. "When your children shall ask their fathers in time to come, saying, What mean these stones?" he says, "then ye shall let your children know, saying, Israel came over this Jordan on dry land. For the Lord your God dried up the waters of Jordan from before you . . . : that all the people of the earth might know the hand of the Lord, that it is mighty: that ye might fear the Lord your God for ever."

Alas, the heap of stones disappeared with the years. So did the memory of what God had done.

STORY 7

The Captain Appears

SAFELY across the Jordan, the children of Israel pitched their tents with a joy in their hearts they had never known before. They were in Canaan at last! Their feet stood upon the Promised Land!

With deep thankfulness to God they kept the Passover, which reminded them of their deliverance from Egypt forty-odd years before. Somehow it seemed to fit in wonderfully with the way God had just led them through the Jordan.

Next morning they ate food they found in Canaan, and the morning after that there was no more manna. The Bible says it "ceased on the morrow after they had eaten of the old corn of the land." No doubt some people, from habit, went out to gather some for breakfast, but there wasn't any. They never saw the manna again. It was just another sign that a new life, a new day, had begun for them.

One day, perhaps as the shades of evening were falling upon the Jordan valley and silence was coming gradually to

85

Before trying to take Jericho Joshua went out of the camp to pray. He did not know he would meet the Captain of the Lord's host, who had come to give him help from heaven.

the camp of Israel, Joshua went off by himself to pray. He was troubled. Better than anyone else he knew the difficulties ahead. Not far away was Jericho, so near he could even see the soldiers on the walls. He wondered how such a city, so strong, so well defended, could be taken by people who knew so little of the arts of war. Beyond Jericho were a hundred other cities just like it, full of fierce, cruel people who would fight to the death to keep Israel from taking them.

Then there were those mountains he could see in the gloaming, so high and steep, barring his way to the sea. How could he take a million people over them?

He told God how helpless he felt, and asked for wisdom that he might know what to do.

Suddenly, as he raised his head, he saw someone standing close by him, a drawn sword in his hand.

No doubt his hand felt for his own sword as he stepped toward the stranger.

"Friend or foe?" he asked, as any soldier would. "Art thou for us, or for our adversaries?"

"Nay," said the stranger, "but as captain of the host of the Lord am I now come."

"The captain of the host!" thought Joshua. Was not *he* the captain? Then the truth dawned upon him. This must be the Lord Himself, the real Captain of Israel. He had come to give him the help, the wisdom, the courage, for which he had prayed.

"And Joshua fell on his face to the earth, and did worship, and said unto him, What saith my lord unto his servant?"

86

THE CAPTAIN APPEARS

The Lord had much to say to him, but first He reminded him to be reverent in the presence of God. Just as He had said to Moses at the burning bush, so now He told Joshua to remove his shoes because the place where he was standing was holy ground. "And Joshua did so."

Then the Lord told him what he most wanted to know—how to capture Jericho. Israel was not to fight at all, but just walk round and round the city. Then everybody was to give a big shout, and the walls would fall down. It would be just as easy as that, if they would only follow God's plan.

How simple the problem seemed to Joshua now! There was no need for him to worry any more. The Captain of the host was in charge, and victory was sure.

So will all our problems become simple if we let the Lord take full charge of our lives.

STORY 8

The Shout That Wrecked a City

THE WATCHMEN on the walls of Jericho were puzzled. Ever since they had seen the children of Israel cross the dry bed of the river they had been expecting an attack. But none had come.

The gates of the city were closed. Every able-bodied man was fully armed, ready for action at a moment's notice. Archers were posted on the battlements to shoot down any attacker. But none came.

Spies reported that the Israelites were going through certain religious ceremonies, but had no big engines of war for dealing with walled cities. Nor were they building any. It was all very strange. Were they planning just to sit there and starve them out?

Then one day they saw a procession forming outside the camp of Israel.

"This must be it," they said to one another, as soldiers were ordered to battle stations. But still the attack did not come.

Instead they saw thousands of armed men—no doubt five in a rank, as they had come out of Egypt—begin to march not *toward* the city, but *around* it. Following them was a group of priests carrying the same strange object they had seen in the midst of Jordan when the Israelites had crossed it. Then came more armed men. And so the procession wound on and on until it had gone completely around the city. Then it went back into the camp of Israel and dispersed.

"That's a funny way to attack a city!" said someone on the walls. "If that's how they mean to make war on us, we won't have much to worry about."

"I don't like it," said another. "Did you notice how quiet they were? Nobody spoke a word, so far as I could hear. The only sound they made was with those trumpets."

Next day the same thing happened—the same procession, the same silent march around the city. It was uncanny.

So it was the next day, and the next. Indeed, for six days in succession.

89

"What are they up to?" many people in the city began to ask. "Do they think they are going to frighten us by just walking round and round like this?"

Then came the seventh day. Early in the morning the procession started again. At first there seemed to be no difference. And there wasn't—until one complete circuit had been made. Then, instead of going back to camp as usual, the soldiers and the priests walked round the city again. Then again and again. Four times, five times, six times. Still not a spear was thrown, not an arrow was shot. And still there was no sound save the noise of the priests' trumpets and the tramp, tramp, tramp of the marching host.

No doubt the walls were thronged with people by now, all watching the amazing sight, wondering what it meant, and what might happen next. Round went the procession for the seventh time.

Suddenly, as the priests blew on their trumpets once more, there was a mighty shout. So loud was it that it seemed as if every soldier in the ranks of the Israelites had shouted at exactly the same moment. The sound wave appeared to strike the walls like a battering ram, for at that precise moment there was a shuddering and a shaking as if an earthquake had hit the city. The great walls began to fall outward. Hundreds of the defenders were tossed to the ground and killed, leaving the city wide open to the Israelites.

Minutes later the fighting was all over. Jericho had been captured. Israel's first victory in Canaan had been won.

PAINTING BY FRED COLLINS

STORY 9

Buried Sin

A S THE Israelites returned to camp after the capture of Jericho, they were very pleased with themselves. They had taken the most important city in the Jordan valley without a fight! All they had had to do was walk around it and shout! It was amazing. They began to think that if all the cities of Canaan could be captured as easily as this, they would possess the land in no time.

Thinking thoughts like these, they set out to take the city of Ai. Because it was much smaller than Jericho, some of the leaders said it would not be necessary for all the men of Israel to go against it. "Let about two or three thousand men go up," they said to Joshua, "and make not all the people to labour thither."

So about three thousand men went up to attack Ai, and were defeated. Thirty-six men were killed, and the rest came home feeling very discouraged.

Something had gone wrong. Joshua felt almost as bad

92

as the rest. He couldn't understand it. Where was the Captain of the Lord's host who had promised victory?

"And Joshua rent his clothes, and fell to the earth upon his face before the ark of the Lord until the eventide, he and the elders of Israel, and put dust upon their heads."

A strange position this for the would-be conqueror of a country, and the Lord didn't like it. "Get thee up," He said to Joshua; "wherefore liest thou thus upon thy face?"

Then the Lord told him what was the matter. Somebody in the camp had committed a grievous sin. Somebody had disobeyed orders and kept part of the spoil of Jericho for himself.

"There is an accursed thing in the midst of thee, O Israel: thou canst not stand before thine enemies, until ye take away the accursed thing from among you."

But how could Joshua find the man who had done this deed? To search for him among a million Israelites would be like looking for a needle in a haystack.

Then the Lord told him to draw lots, first to find the tribe to which the man belonged, then to find his family, and finally to find the man himself.

Meanwhile, Achan, who had stolen the stuff and buried it in his tent, felt perfectly safe.

"They'll never catch me," he told himself. "Never."

Even when Joshua called all the people together and began to draw lots, Achan didn't feel worried. Amid so many, many thousands of people, how could they ever find him— especially when nobody in the camp knew what he had done?

But when he heard that in the casting of lots for the twelve tribes, the tribe of Judah had been taken, he became a little anxious. "That's my tribe," he told himself. "But then think of all the thousands of families in Judah. I'm still all right."

But he became more worried when he learned that as lots were cast among the families of Judah, the family of the Zarhites had been taken.

"That's my family," he said. "I don't like this. It's getting too close."

Minutes later the search came closer still, for Zabdi, Achan's grandfather, was taken. As the old man went forward to speak with Joshua, and the priests began to cast lots on Zabdi's children and grandchildren, Achan's face turned pale.

Then he heard his own name called, and his heart sank. He knew then the game was up.

"My son," said Joshua, kindly but solemnly, "give, I pray thee, glory to the Lord God of Israel, and make confession unto him; and tell me now what thou hast done; hide it not from me."

Trembling, Achan confessed. There was nothing else he could do. Yes, he was the one who had sinned. When Jericho was captured he had seen "a goodly Babylonish garment," which he thought it would be nice to wear someday, and two hundred shekels of silver and a wedge of gold. "I coveted them and took them," he said, "and, behold, they are hid in the earth in the midst of my tent."

Joshua sent men to Achan's tent and soon found the goods and brought them back. They made a sad little pile in front of Joshua and the elders of Israel, and the Babylonish garment didn't look nearly so beautiful as before. What a shame that Israel had suffered defeat in battle, and many good men had been killed, because of this flimsy piece of cloth and a few bits of silver and gold!

Achan was sorry, terribly sorry. But it was too late to be sorry. He had to be punished. And he was.

He was taken to a valley where there were many stones, and the people threw stones at him till he died. "And they raised over him a great heap of stones unto this day."

The place was called Achor, meaning "trouble." And what a lot of trouble was caused by that one little sin, a buried sin that wouldn't stay covered!

STORY 10

Moldy Bread

WHEN Achan had been punished Ai was easily taken. Not with three thousand men, though. All the people of war went up against it, just as they had against Jericho, and the city was sacked and burned.

As news of this second great victory spread through the land, the people of Canaan became very frightened. Some of the rulers of the larger cities decided to band together and wage war on Israel. Others thought it would be better to make a treaty of peace with the invaders, if that were possible. Among these were the leading men of Gibeon who thought up quite a bright idea to save themselves.

Their city was not very far from Ai, and they guessed that if they did not do something soon, it might be their turn to be destroyed next. So they dressed themselves up as ambassadors from a far country, "and took old sacks upon their asses, and wine bottles, old, and rent, and bound up; and old shoes . . . upon their feet, and old garments upon them; and

96

all the bread . . . was dry and mouldy. And they went to Joshua unto the camp at Gilgal, and said unto him, and to the men of Israel, We be come from a far country: now therefore make ye a league with us."

Some of the leaders of Israel were a bit suspicious of the travel-stained strangers, and looked them over very carefully, but none detected the fraud. So Joshua asked them who they were and whence they had come.

Wearily they answered, "From a very far country thy servants are come because of the name of the Lord thy God: for we have heard the fame of him, and all that he did in Egypt, and all that he did to the two kings of the Amorites, that were beyond Jordan, to Sihon king of Heshbon and to Og king of Bashan."

Carefully they avoided mentioning Jericho and Ai, which would have given them away.

Then, seeing that their speech had made a big impression on Joshua and the princes of Israel, they went on to point to the food they had brought with them.

"This our bread," they said sadly, "we took hot . . . out of our houses on the day we came forth to go unto you; but now, behold, it is dry, and it is mouldy: and these bottles of wine, which we filled, were new; and, behold, they be rent: and these our garments and our shoes are become old by reason of the very long journey."

How they kept their faces straight while they told all these untruths, I can't imagine. But they did. And Joshua believed them. So did the other leaders who listened to them. How could they deny the evidence of that moldy bread? "And Joshua made peace with them, and made a league with them, to let them live: and the princes of the congregation sware unto them."

Of course it wasn't long before the fraud was discovered. In fact, within three days the truth was out. You can imagine how foolish and angry Joshua and the others felt about it. But they kept their word. When they came to Gibeon they left it unharmed. However, as a punishment for their deception, the Gibeonites were told that they must forever be "hewers of wood and drawers of water" for the children of Israel.

How did it happen that Joshua and the princes of Israel were deceived by these cunning people? The Bible says, "They received the men by reason of their victuals, and asked not counsel at the mouth of the Lord."

God was ready to give them counsel on this matter, just as He had given them counsel on how to take Jericho and Ai. But being perhaps a bit puffed up over their two great victories, they had thought it wasn't necessary to ask God about such a little matter as this. So they were deceived by a piece of moldy bread.

It is a good thing to take every question to God and let Him guide in every detail of our lives.

STORY 11

The Sun Stands Still

≈≈≈≈≈≈≈≈≈≈≈≈≈≈≈≈≈≈≈≈≈

THAT piece of moldy bread the Gibeonites showed to Joshua brought him more trouble than he expected.

Not long after he had signed the treaty with them they sent him an urgent message asking for help. They were about to be attacked by five kings of nearby cities, and would he please come at once and save them?

"Come up to us quickly, and save us, and help us," they pleaded: "for all the kings of the Amorites . . . are gathered together against us."

These five kings had planned to attack the Israelites and stop their invasion of Canaan, so, naturally, when they heard the Gibeonites had made peace with Israel they were very angry. Traitors, they called them, and set out to punish them. Hence the Gibeonites appealed to Joshua for help.

This time Joshua did not forget to ask God what to do. To his surprise the Lord told him to go to the help of these people who had deceived him—and to go at once.

99

By marching all night the armies of Israel reached Gibeon just in time. Taken by surprise, the soldiers of the five kings scattered in all directions.

During the fighting that followed two wonderful things happened. First came a sudden storm of hail which beat down the enemy so that "they were more which died with hailstones than they whom the children of Israel slew with the sword."

Then, as the pursuit continued toward evening, and Joshua saw that many would escape in the oncoming darkness, he prayed for more time to finish the job.

He realized that this was a most important battle. If he won it, he would break the power of the Canaanites once and for all. His path to the sea would be open, and to all Canaan too. He *must* win it. Oh, for more daylight! If only the sun would not go down!

Suddenly he looked toward the setting sun and cried, "Sun, stand thou still upon Gibeon; and thou, Moon, in the valley of Ajalon."

Just how it happened I do not know, but the Bible says that "the sun stood still, and the moon stayed" until the battle was won.

Hour after hour, when normally there would have been darkness, there was light. The sun continued to shine. In fact, the sun "hasted not to go down about a whole day." It just stayed where it was in the sky. "And there was no day like that before it or after it, that the Lord hearkened unto the voice of a man: for the Lord fought for Israel."

100

Of course, everybody in Palestine knew about this and marveled at the long, long day. And when they heard that it had happened just so Israel could defeat the five kings, they had little fight left in them. In the battles that followed Israel had one succession of victories. "So Joshua took the whole land, according to all that the Lord said unto Moses."

At last, when all the fighting was over, Joshua carefully divided the land among the people of Israel. To make sure everybody would be satisfied, he set up a committee of twenty-one men who explored the whole country and "described it by cities into seven parts in a book." With this book beside him he cast lots for the land, and the various tribes accepted the portions that came to them. Then they all set off to start their new life in the Promised Land.

"There failed not ought of any good thing which the Lord had spoken unto the house of Israel; all came to pass."

STORY 12

Joshua's Last Days

WHEN the land of Canaan was being divided among the tribes of Israel, two beautiful things happened.

The first was when old Caleb came to make a request. What do you suppose this eighty-five-year-old veteran asked for? A nice, flat piece of fertile land by the Jordan? No, indeed. Not he. "Give me this mountain," he said, pointing to the one where the giant sons of Anak still lived. "If so be the Lord will be with me, then I shall be able to drive them out."

It was these very sons of Anak who had frightened the people forty years before. Now Caleb, brave to the last, offered to meet them in battle himself. He did, and he won.

Then, when the dividing of the land was almost over, Joshua's turn came. What did he request? As leader he might have demanded a very large and beautiful tract of land, but he didn't. Instead he asked for one little ruined city, which he had to rebuild. And when it was given to him he called it

102

JOSHUA'S LAST DAYS

Timnath-serah, meaning "the portion that remains." Here was the mark of a truly great man. He took nothing for himself until everybody else had been cared for.

Years passed by. Years of peace and joy for Israel. Joshua passed his hundredth birthday. Soon after this, feeling that his end was near, he called all the people together as Moses had done just before he died. When they came to him he reminded them again of all God's goodness to them from the day He called Abraham out of Ur of the Chaldees. Carrying their minds back to the days of their bondage in Egypt, he spoke of the great deliverance at the Red Sea, of the miraculous crossing of the Jordan, and lastly of all the wonderful victories God had given them since that day.

"Take good heed therefore unto yourselves, that ye love the Lord your God," he implored them. "Fear the Lord, and serve him in sincerity and in truth."

Then he warned them of what would happen if they should ever forget the God who had blessed them so, adding those last wonderful words of his: "Choose you this day whom ye will serve . . . : as for me and my house, we will serve the Lord."

Deeply touched by their old leader's faith and his deep concern for them, the people replied, "The Lord our God we will serve, and his voice will we obey."

They meant it. I am sure they did. And as long as Joshua lived they kept their word.

Then Joshua died, "being an hundred and ten years old." And where do you suppose they buried him? In his own little city of Timnath-serah, "the portion that remains"—a fitting place for one whose name will remain forever.

PART III

Stories of the Judges

(JUDGES 1:1-RUTH 4:22)

BALAAM MET
BY THE ANGEL

WALLED CITIES OF
THE CANAANITES

SEA
OF
GALILEE

BAAL WORSHIP

MT. EBAL

MT. GERIZIM

TABERNACLE
AT SHILOH

RIVER JABBOK

TENT CITIES

LAND OF GIANTS

CROSSING
THE JORDAN

RIVER ARNON

THE FALL OF JERICHO

GIBEONITES

DEAD
SEA

SETTLEMENT OF CANAAN
UNDER JOSHUA'S LEADERSHIP

QUADE

STORY   1

The Place of Weepers

WHEN the tribes of Israel were given the land of Canaan, it was with the understanding that they were to drive out the rest of the wicked people they found there, smash their idols, and break down their altars. They were to create in Palestine a pure and holy nation that would glow with the glory of God in an evil world. But they didn't do it. They got tired too soon.

Eager to build homes for themselves and begin farming again, they found all sorts of excuses for not doing exactly what God, through Joshua, had told them to do.

The tribe of Judah, we read, drove out "the inhabitants of the mountain; but could not drive out the inhabitants of the valley, because they had chariots of iron." But what had chariots of iron to do with it? Could not God have found a way to deal with them, as He had helped Israel through the Red Sea and Jordan?

The first chapter of Judges is one long story of failure.

107

After crossing the Jordan and overcoming the giants in their walled cities, the Israelites set up their tabernacle, made friends with Gibeon, and richly prospered as God had promised.

"Neither did Manasseh drive out the inhabitants of Beth-shean."

"Neither did Ephraim drive out the Canaanites that dwelt in Gezer."

"Neither did Zebulun drive out the inhabitants of Kitron."

And so on and so on. Then it says, "The Amorites forced the children of Dan into the mountain: for they would not suffer them to come down to the valley." What a shameful thing to happen after all the smashing victories Israel had had under Joshua!

It was all very disappointing.

What God thought about it is revealed in the words of "the angel of the Lord" who came to speak to the children of Israel at a place called Bochim.

"I made you to go up out of Egypt," he said sadly, "and have brought you unto the land which I sware unto your fathers; and I said, I will never break my covenant with you. And ye shall make no league with the inhabitants of this land; ye shall throw down their altars: but ye have not obeyed my voice: why have ye done this?"

Then He reminded them of the warning given through Moses long before: "Wherefore I also said, I will not drive them out from before you; but they shall be as thorns in your sides, and their gods shall be a snare unto you."

As the children of Israel listened to these solemn words of rebuke and warning, they became very sad indeed. They knew that this messenger from heaven was telling the truth. They had failed to do as God had told them. They hadn't driven out the Canaanites. They hadn't destroyed their idols. They hadn't broken down their altars. They had been lazy, selfish, stupid, disobedient. And now God wasn't going to help them any more.

First one began to cry, then another and another until everybody was in tears. "All the children of Israel . . . lifted up their voice, and wept. And they called the name of that place Bochim," which means the "place of weepers."

It was good that they wept. God was pleased to see that they were sorry for their sins. The pity is that their repentance didn't last very long. All too soon they again "did evil in the sight of the Lord, and served Baalim: and they forsook the Lord God of their fathers, which brought them out of the land of Egypt, and followed other gods. . . .

"And the anger of the Lord was hot against Israel, and he delivered them into the hands of spoilers that spoiled them, and he sold them into the hands of their enemies round about. . . . Whithersoever they went out, the hand of the Lord was against them for evil, as the Lord had said, and as the Lord had sworn unto them: and they were greatly distressed."

Sad, sad day!

.It is hard to think that people who had seen the Lord do so many wonderful things for them could forget Him so quickly. But they did. And what a price they had to pay! Before long every city they had built, every home they dwelt in, became a Bochim, a "place of weepers."

What a lesson for us all! May we never forget the Lord!

STORY 2

Seesaw Days

FOR MANY years after the death of Joshua the fortunes of the people of Israel were like a seesaw. Sometimes they were up. Sometimes they were down.

When the people forgot God and worshiped the idols of Canaan, great trouble came upon them; when they turned back to God, good times came again.

It was just like that—seesaw, seesaw. And what a pity! For God had planned such a wonderful time for them. He wanted them to "ride upon the high places of the earth" always. He wanted them to be the greatest, noblest nation that ever was, telling all the world about His love. But, alas, "they forsook the Lord, and served Baal," and great evil came upon them.

"Nevertheless," the Bible says, "the Lord raised up judges, which delivered them out of the hand of those that spoiled them." But "when the judge was dead, . . . they returned, and corrupted themselves more than their fathers, in follow-

110

ing other gods to serve them, and to bow down to them; they ceased not from their own doings, nor from their stubborn way."

That was the story—seesaw, seesaw, down and up—turning away from God into trouble and turning from trouble back to God.

The first punishment came when God allowed the king of Mesopotamia to invade the land. This man kept Israel in bondage for eight long years. At last, when they were sorry for their sins and cried to God for deliverance, He helped Othniel, Caleb's nephew, to drive out the invader. With his uncle's brave spirit he roused the people and led them to victory.

For forty years after that all went well, but after Othniel died the people forgot God again and "did evil in the sight of the Lord." So He let Eglon, king of Moab, take the country, and Israel spent eighteen years under another foreign king.

By and by they became sorry they had done wrong, and the Lord forgave them. This time he sent a man called Ehud to rescue them. He won a great victory over Moab, and there was peace for eighty years. "And the children of Israel again did evil in the sight of the Lord, when Ehud was dead. And the Lord sold them into the hand of Jabin king of Canaan."

They were just like some little children I know: so naughty that they have to be spanked; then sorry for their sins; then good for a little while; then naughty all over again. Maybe you know somebody like that.

It was just too bad, for not only was God's beautiful purpose spoiled but everybody was kept so miserable and poor. The invaders stole their crops and their money, and made them work for nothing.

When Jabin, king of Canaan, came, the Bible says "he mightily oppressed the children of Israel." That must have been a very bad time. But again when the people were sorry for their sins, the Lord had pity on them and sent Deborah to help them. She was "a mother in Israel" and a prophetess. She stirred all Israel to go and fight Sisera, the captain of Jabin's army, even though he did have nine hundred chariots of iron. Led by this very brave woman, Israel won a great victory, Sisera himself being killed by a woman named Jael while he was asleep.

"Praise ye the Lord for the avenging of Israel," sang Deborah after the battle. And the people did praise Him. They were so glad to be free again. "So let all thine enemies perish, O Lord," they cried; "but let them that love him be as the sun when he goeth forth in his might."

It seemed for a while as if a great revival was about to sweep over the land. The watching angels must have thought that perhaps at last Israel had learned their lesson; from now on maybe God would be able to bless them as He so much wanted to do. But no; it was not to be. What looked like sunrise became sunset all too soon. Once again "the children of Israel did evil in the sight of the Lord: and the Lord delivered them into the hand of Midian."

How sad that a whole people should turn away from God so easily! We must pray that we never do the same.

STORY 3

An Angel Burns the Dinner

AFTER seven years under the rule of the Midianites, things became so bad for the people of Israel that they fled from their homes and lived in dens and caves in the mountains. When some of the bravest ventured out to sow their seed in the fields, enemy soldiers would destroy it before it was full grown, so that there was left "no sustenance for Israel, neither sheep, nor ox, nor ass." Everybody was starving.

The worst days in the wilderness were never so bad as these. How the poor Israelites must have longed for Moses and Joshua! It seemed as if God had utterly forsaken them. But He hadn't. In fact, "his soul was grieved for the misery of Israel." He was always looking for the first sign that they were sorry for their sins, and for someone through whom He could deliver them.

This time He found a man in a little place called Ophrah. Here on a hot summer afternoon a youth was threshing wheat

115

When God needed a brave leader on whom
He could depend to deliver the Israelites from
the Midianites, He sent an angel to call
Gideon, who was threshing wheat at Ophrah.

by the wine press "to hide it from the Midianites." Since it wasn't time for the grape harvest, he thought they wouldn't be looking around the wine press for a while.

Though he was tall, strong, and good looking, resembling "the children of a king," this young man's heart was sad as he thought of the sorrows of his people. Surely, it seemed, life was hardly worth living.

Suddenly, looking up from his work, he was startled to see a stranger sitting under a nearby oak. He had been sure that he was alone, hidden from all prying eyes. But no. Someone was looking at him. Who could it be? A Midianite?

The stranger spoke. "The Lord is with thee, thou mighty man of valour."

So! Then he must be a friend.

"Oh my Lord," said Gideon, pouring out all that was on his heart, "if the Lord be with us, why then is all this befallen us? and where be all his miracles which our fathers told us of, saying, Did not the Lord bring us up from Egypt? but now the Lord hath forsaken us."

The stranger then looked straight at him, right into his eyes, and said, "Go in this thy might, and thou shalt save Israel from the hand of the Midianites."

"I?" said Gideon, with the same humility that Moses had shown when God called him at the burning bush. "Oh my Lord, wherewith shall I save Israel? behold, my family is poor . . . , and I am the least in my father's house."

"And the Lord said unto him, Surely I will be with thee, and thou shalt smite the Midianites as one man."

116

Gideon could hardly believe his ears. He wondered whether he might be dreaming. "Show me a sign that you are really talking with me," he said to the stranger. Then he remembered that he should be hospitable. "Please wait until I bring some food."

All excited, he ran to his humble home, cooked some meat, boiled some broth, and baked some fresh cakes—all very scarce and precious at that time. Then he hurried back to the oak, wondering whether his visitor would still be there.

He was. And to Gideon's surprise he told him to put the meat and the cakes on a nearby rock and pour out the broth.

Gideon did as he was told, though it must have seemed a dreadful waste.

The stranger then touched the food with the end of the staff that was in his hand, "and there rose up fire out of the

117

rock, and consumed the flesh and the unleavened cakes." Then he vanished.

Now Gideon was sure his visitor had been none other than an angel of the Lord. Bowing his head he cried, "Alas, O Lord God! . . . because I have seen an angel of the Lord face to face."

"Peace be unto thee," whispered the Lord to him; "fear not: thou shalt not die."

Deeply moved, Gideon's first thought was to build an altar to the God of heaven, the God of Abraham, Isaac, and Jacob, who had spoken to him in this place. So he piled stones upon the rock where the fire had blazed, and called the place "Jehovah-shalom," meaning "the Lord send peace."

That prayer was the longing of his heart. The Lord wanted to send peace, but there was much else to be done.

STORY 4

The Wet-dry Fleece

THAT very night the Lord spoke to Gideon again, telling him just what he was to do. He was to begin his task at once, and at home. The first step to driving the Midianites out of the country was to throw down the altar of Baal in his own back yard.

So, in the dead of night, taking ten of his young friends to help him, Gideon broke down the altar of Baal that his father had built. Before sunrise it was in pieces, and the grove of trees around it cut down.

Next he sent messengers throughout the land calling for volunteers to help him fight the Midianites. Thousands flocked to him.

But he was still worried about his call. Had God really spoken to him? Would He stand by him in the battles ahead?

He decided to ask God to show him very clearly that there had been no mistake.

Taking a "fleece of wool," he laid it on the earth. Then

119

he said to God that if in the morning the dew had fallen only on the fleece, while the earth around it was dry, he would know that all was well and that God really did want him to save Israel from the Midianites.

In the morning the fleece was so wet that Gideon wrung a bowlful of water out of it, and the earth about it was dry.

But still he had a lingering doubt. The fleece *might* have become damp from the moisture in the air. To make quite sure, he asked God to give him one more sign. Tomorrow morning, he said, "let it now be dry only upon the fleece, and upon all the ground let there be dew."

"And God did so that night: for it was dry upon the fleece only, and there was dew on all the ground."

As Gideon picked up the dry fleece from the sodden earth, all doubt left his mind. I can see him standing there alone, with his head bowed, saying, "Thank you, dear Lord. I'm ready now. I know everything will be all right."

STORY 5

Three Hundred Heroes

MORE and more of the men of Israel found their way to the place where Gideon had raised the standard of revolt against the Midianites, until he had an army of thirty-two thousand.

"You have too many," said the Lord.

"Too many!" This was hard for any army commander to understand.

"That's right," the Lord told him; "it's too dangerous to fight with so many lest the people should take the glory of the victory to themselves."

At the Lord's command, and to everybody's surprise, Gideon said to the crowd of men around him, "Whosoever is fearful and afraid, let him return and depart."

To Gideon's dismay he saw his army melt away. Twenty-two thousand men went home!

I imagine he said, "This is impossible. With only ten thousand men left, perhaps we had better give up the whole idea."

121

But the Lord said, "Gideon, the people are yet too many."
Still too many! How could it be?

Then the Lord told him to take the ten thousand men he had left over to a nearby stream, and He would point out which of them should go into battle.

When all were gathered at the water's edge the Lord told Gideon that all who went down on their knees to drink should be sent home. Only those who brought the water to their mouths with their hands, and lapped it "as a dog lappeth," were to remain.

When it was all over, how many soldiers do you suppose Gideon had left? Just three hundred. And why were they chosen? It could be because, unlike all the others, they did not bend their heads when they drank, but kept their eyes on the enemy every moment. They were the only ones who were really eager to fight.

Now what to do? How could Gideon hope to defeat the great host of Midianites with such a handful, brave and devoted though they might be?

122

THREE HUNDRED HEROES

When the Lord saw how worried Gideon was He said to him, "By the three hundred men . . . will I save you."

And so it happened. The Lord told Gideon to give each man a trumpet, a torch, and an empty pitcher. At the right moment the torch was to be lighted and hidden inside the pitcher.

Under cover of darkness Gideon placed his men in three companies around the camp of the Midianites. Then in the middle of the night, at a signal from him, each man broke his pitcher, revealing the flaming torch. Then all blew their trumpets and shouted at the top of their voices, "The sword of the Lord, and of Gideon."

The sleeping Midianites awoke with a start and, seeing the torches and hearing loud shouts all around them, presumed that the Israelites were attacking them from all sides. Losing their heads, they struck out right and left, killing one another by thousands. The rest fled, with the three hundred heroes chasing them, "faint, yet pursuing."

A great victory was won, as great as any in Israel's history.

It showed that God was still ready to help His people, still able to save them, by many or by few.

STORY 6

Saddest Little Girl

THERE have been many sad little girls in the world, but this story is about the saddest of them all.

We do not know her name—only that she was the daughter of a man called Jephthah, one of the men whom God raised up to help Israel after the death of Gideon.

She was an only child, for Jephthah, though "a mighty man of valour," had no sons and only one daughter.

Although she had no brothers or sisters, I am sure she loved her daddy very much, and I know he dearly loved her. Maybe, like most little girls, she dreamed that someday, when she was grown up, she would get married and have boys and girls of her own. Somehow that would make up for feeling so lonesome as a child.

Well, one day when her daddy went out to fight the Ammonites, who had threatened to take away much of Israel's land, he made a strange vow. He promised the Lord that if he should win the battle, he would give Him the first thing

124

that came out of his house to meet him on his return. Of course, he expected that it would be one of the animals which, in those days, for safety's sake, people kept in their houses. He thought it might be a lamb, or a kid, or a calf, which he would gladly offer up as a burnt offering.

Imagine his feelings when, returning from victory over the Ammonites, he saw running toward him, not an animal, but his own precious daughter!

At any other time he would have been overjoyed to see her. She looked so sweet and pretty, with tambourines in her hands, dancing down the hillside toward him, singing for joy like any other little girl who loved her daddy.

But poor Jephthah was heartbroken. To her amazement he burst into tears and tore his clothes, as people did in those days when they were very upset about something.

"What's the matter, Daddy," I can hear her saying, "aren't you glad to see me?"

Then he told her about the vow he had made, and how he never dreamed that she would be the one to come to meet him. I imagine they just cried and cried in each other's arms!

Of course, he couldn't offer up his daughter as a burnt offering, but he had to keep his vow to give her to the Lord. His friends would have thought him very wicked if he had broken his word. So he said she must never marry, but serve the Lord as a single girl all her life.

It was very hard for her to take. She had so wanted to have those boys and girls of her own that she had dreamed about. Now she never could.

With some of her girl friends she went up into the mountains to cry about it. Together they stayed there for two long, dreary months. Afterward, when she was home again, they came to talk and weep with her four days every year. That's why I think she was one of the saddest little girls in history.

STORY 7

Much-wanted Boy

HIS MOTHER wanted him, his father wanted him, but most of all God wanted him.

Manoah and his wife had longed for a little boy, but no baby came. Then one day a messenger from God met the woman and told her that she would have a son and that she must dedicate him to God from the day of his birth because God had a great work for him to do. He wanted him to become a leader in Israel and save His people from the Philistines, who now ruled over them.

On reaching home she told her husband what had happened. "A man of God came unto me," she said, "and his countenance was like the countenance of an angel of God, very terrible: but I asked him not whence he was, neither told he me his name: but he said unto me, Behold, thou shalt conceive, and bear a son; and now drink no wine nor strong drink, neither any unclean thing: for the child shall be a Nazarite to God . . . to the day of his death."

Manoah did not question his wife's story, but bowed in prayer, saying, "O my Lord, let the man of God which thou didst send come again unto us, and teach us what we shall do unto the child that shall be born."

That was a very beautiful prayer, and the Lord heard it. The man of God came again and gave them both the same advice he had given before.

After they had talked together for a while about the baby, Manoah offered to bring the visitor a meal, but he declined. However, he said that if Manoah would like to offer a sacrifice to God, that would be all right. So Manoah took the kid that he was going to prepare for food and offered it as a burnt offering. As he did so, something very wonderful happened. Suddenly, as the fire rose around the sacrifice, the man of God vanished, ascending toward heaven in the flames.

Startled, Manoah and his wife "fell on their faces to the ground," sure that they had seen an angel of the Lord.

Manoah was scared that both of them would die, but his wife was more sensible. No, she said, if the Lord had wanted to kill them both, He would not have accepted their offering, nor would He have sent an angel to tell them all about the baby.

She was right, and by and by the baby boy arrived, just as the angel had said.

Proudly and thankfully they called his name Samson. "And the child grew, and the Lord blessed him."

With what loving care did those two dear people watch over their little boy! With what eager hope did they look forward to the day when he would be a grown man, ready to do the great work God wanted him to do!

Alas, how bitterly disappointed they were to be!

STORY 8

Strongest Man That Ever Lived

SAMSON became the strongest man that ever lived. Thanks to the loving care his parents gave him, he grew to be so big and powerful that nobody could stand before him. Once when but a youth he tore a young lion apart with his bare hands.

But though he was strong of body, he was also selfish and headstrong and a great problem to his father and mother.

As he was growing up, he fell in love with a Philistine maiden and wanted to marry her right away. Naturally his parents tried to persuade him not to do such a thing. "Can't you find a wife among your own people?" they said to him, kindly but earnestly. "Why take one from among our enemies?"

But Samson wouldn't listen to them. "Get her for me," he said; "for she pleaseth me well."

So he married her. And what a lot of trouble and sorrow it brought to them all!

One day as he happened to pass the carcass of the lion

130

he had killed, he noticed that there was a swarm of bees with honey in it. This gave him an idea for a bit of fun at his wedding feast. There were thirty young men there as guests, and he asked them the meaning of this riddle: "Out of the eater came forth meat, and out of the strong came forth sweetness." Then he offered to give them each a suit of clothes if they could give the answer during the seven days of the feast. If they failed to answer in that time, they were to give him thirty suits.

Unable to guess the riddle, the young men began to get worried. They were afraid they would all have to give their own clothes to Samson, and then what would they do?

On the seventh day they came to Samson's wife and persuaded her to try to find out the meaning of the riddle. She pleaded with him to tell her, and in a moment of weakness he did. Then she told the young men, and they came to Samson and said, "What is sweeter than honey? and what is stronger than a lion?"

Samson was so angry that his wife had told his secret that he went and killed thirty Philistines and brought their clothes and gave them to the thirty young men. Then—after being with his wife only seven days—he left her in a huff and went back to his old home.

When he had cooled down a bit he decided to go back to

131

his wife, but found that she had married someone else, thinking he didn't love her any more. At this he was furious. To take revenge, he caught three hundred foxes, tied them together in pairs, tail to tail, with a firebrand in between, then let the maddened animals loose in the cornfields and vineyards of the Philistines. You can imagine what happened. Those foxes must have set fire to hundreds of acres, leaving only blackened fields behind them.

Now it was the Philistines' turn to get angry. They marched into the land of Judah and demanded that Samson be handed over to them for punishment. So three thousand men of Judah surrounded Samson, bound him, and gave him to the Philistines. But no sooner was he back among his enemies than he broke his bonds as though they were "flax that was burnt with fire" and, picking up the jawbone of an ass, slew a thousand men with it.

By this time his fame as the strongest man on earth was spreading. Everybody was afraid of him. Try as they would, the Philistines could not catch him. One night when he was in Gaza the rulers of the city shut the gates so that he couldn't get away. But at midnight Samson carried away both gates and gateposts and dumped them on the top of a hill some miles away!

Next morning, when the Philistines saw that great gap in the walls of Gaza, they must have had a shock. But what could they do? This giant of a man was just too strong and too smart for them.

Then they heard that Samson had fallen in love with a woman named Delilah, and they made up their minds to work through her to get him. "Find the secret of his strength," they begged her, and in her sly way she tried to do so. But it wasn't easy. Three times he deceived her.

Once he told her that if she bound him with seven fresh bowstrings, he would be helpless. But when she had tied him up he snapped them in a moment.

Another time he said that if she bound him with new ropes, he would be as weak as other men. But when she had gone to all the trouble of finding new ropes and tying him up with them, he broke them as if they had been thread.

The third time he told her—for fun—that if she were to weave his hair in with the cloth she was making, he would never be able to get free. So that night while he was asleep she did that very thing. But in the morning he walked off with all the weaving machinery hanging from his head, and laughed at her.

Day after day she asked him to tell her his secret, pouting and fussing and teasing until "his soul was vexed unto death."

133

In other words, she kept it up until he felt he couldn't stand it any longer. Then he told her.

The secret of his strength, he said, lay in the fact that he was a Nazarite, a man dedicated to God, the sign of which was his long, beautiful hair, done up in seven long locks. If these seven locks should ever be cut off, he said, he would really become weak as other men.

Feeling sure that he had told her the truth at last, Delilah planned to cut off his hair that very night, and invited the lords of the Philistines to come up and see the result.

After Samson had fallen asleep she had a man shave his head. The seven golden locks, symbol of his devotion to God, fell to the floor and his strength went with them.

"The Philistines be upon thee, Samson," she cried, but he couldn't do a thing about it. He tried to put up a fight, but "the Lord was departed from him."

Now he was made a prisoner. The Philistines put out his eyes, bound him with fetters of brass, and set him to work in a treadmill.

Poor Samson! What a miserable failure he had made of everything! It is hard to think that that blind, fettered man in the treadmill was once that little boy his parents had loved so dearly, and of whom God had expected so much. How old Manoah and his wife must have wept over him and wished somehow they might have stopped him from going with those heathen girls! But it was too late now.

As that treadmill went round and round and round, Samson had time to think of all his mistakes and the life he might have lived. In shame and sorrow he turned back to God and pleaded for one more chance.

As week after week and month after month went by, he noticed that his hair was growing again. And every inch it grew seemed to bring him closer to God. Gradually he felt his old strength coming back.

Then one day he was let out of the treadmill. He heard people talking about a great feast to Dagon, god of the Philistines. Someone told him that he had been released so he could "make sport" for the merrymakers. Then he guessed where he was being taken. He had been to the place before. He remembered that there were two great pillars in the center supporting the roof. An idea came to him. He asked the lad who was leading him by the hand to show him where the pillars were, so he could lean upon them.

Once there, he put an arm around each pillar and cried from the depths of his soul, "O Lord God, remember me, I

135

pray thee, and strengthen me, I pray thee, only this once, O God, that I may at once be avenged of the Philistines for my two eyes." Resting for a moment between the pillars he prayed he might die with his enemies.

Then he "bowed himself with all his might," heaving and tugging at the pillars. Suddenly there was an awful rending noise as they toppled and fell. Then the whole place came crashing down upon him, together with three thousand people who had been sitting on the roof. "So the dead which he slew at his death were more than they which he slew in his life."

So died Samson, the strongest man who ever lived—the man who, had he tried to please God instead of himself, might have been one of the greatest men of history.

STORY 9

Gleaner Girl

OUT OF all the darkness and sadness of the days when Israel was ruled by the judges comes one of the sweetest stories ever told.

It is about a little girl called Ruth, who belonged to the Moabites, long-time enemies of Israel.

As a child I suppose she heard only bad things about the Israelites, and she might always have disliked them but for the fact that she met Naomi.

Naomi was the mother of two boys about Ruth's age. One was called Mahlon, the other, Chilion. Their father's name was Elimelech and the four of them had come all the way from Bethlehem to Moab because of a famine in their own country.

After Elimelech's death Ruth and Mahlon fell in love and married, and a girl friend of Ruth's named Orpah, married Chilion.

The five of them were very happy together, for Naomi

◄— PAINTING BY KREIGH COLLINS   © 1954, BY REVIEW AND HERALD

God answered Samson's prayer and gave him
strength to destroy the temple of the fish-god
Dagon and three thousand Philistines who had
mocked him and oppressed the people of Israel.

was the nicest mother-in-law any girl could wish to have. She loved her daughters-in-law dearly, and they loved her just as much.

A godly woman, she was no doubt very sorry when her sons married heathen girls, but she made up her mind to lead them, if she could, to love the God of Israel.

Taking every chance to tell them of God's love, as she had heard the story from her parents long before, she told them how He created the world in the beginning and made of it a beautiful home for man, how Adam and Eve sinned and lost their garden home, and how God planned to give it back to them someday. She told them too about the Flood and the rescue of Noah and his family in the ark, of God's promises to Abraham, the dark days in Egypt, the great deliverance in the days of Moses, and all God had done for His people since.

Ruth and Orpah loved to listen as Naomi talked to them, and especially when she told of the wonderful things she believed God would do for Israel in the future. Someday, she may have said, through some sweet girl, "the seed of the woman" would come to bruise the serpent's head.

Ten years passed by. Then trouble came, and great sorrow. First Mahlon died, then Chilion, one after the other.

The sadness in that home must have been terrible, with Naomi, Ruth, and Orpah all crying at once over the loss of their loved ones. Poor things! How hard it must have been for them to believe in the goodness of God! But they did.

Brave Naomi decided she would go back to her old home

in Bethlehem, and the two girls said they would go with her. On the way, however, Naomi worried about them. She wondered whether she was doing right in taking them away from their own country. Perhaps they would be better off if they were to go back to their mothers.

"Go, return each to her mother's house," she said to them kindly: "the Lord deal kindly with you, as ye have dealt with the dead, and with me." Then she kissed them, and they all burst out crying again.

Both Ruth and Orpah said they would rather stay with her than go back to their homeland. They wouldn't leave her. They loved her too much. But Naomi said it was better that they should go back. They must find new husbands, she said, and it would be easier to do this where they were known, among their own people.

They talked for a long time about it, and then Orpah decided that maybe Naomi was right. So she said good-by with many tears and went back home. I can see her waving her last farewell before fading from sight round a bend in the road.

But Ruth wouldn't go. Instead she said to Naomi, in words

that will live forever, "Intreat me not to leave thee . . . for whither thou goest, I will go; and where thou lodgest, I will lodge: thy people shall be my people, and thy God my God."

So Naomi and Ruth went on their way together, trudging slowly and sadly up the rough, steep mountain trail that led to Bethlehem.

When they came at last to the ancient village there was great excitement. "Naomi is back!" the people cried, crowding around to hear the news she brought from the land of Moab. "But where is your husband?" they asked. And, "Where are the boys?" Tearfully she told her story. "I went out full, and the Lord hath brought me home again empty."

Fortunately the barley harvest was just beginning, so there was work to do and food to eat. Ruth at once offered to go into the fields and glean with the other village girls. In those days

140

grain was cut and gathered by hand, and what was left by the reapers had to be picked up by the gleaners.

One day as she was busily at work, Boaz, the owner of the field, came by. Seeing a strange girl among his gleaners, he stopped to ask who she was.

The man in charge replied, "It is the Moabitish damsel that came back with Naomi out of the country of Moab."

Boaz was interested. He had wanted to meet her, especially since Naomi was a relative of his.

Calling Ruth to him, he told her he had heard of all her kindness to Naomi, and how she had willingly left her own country to come and live among strangers. "The Lord recompense thy work, and a full reward be given thee of the Lord God of Israel, under whose wings thou art come to trust."

Smiling sweetly, Ruth thanked him for his gracious words;

and Boaz, very pleased with her, told the reapers to let some of the sheaves drop where she could glean them, so that she would have lots of grain to take home to Naomi.

As the days went by, Boaz and Ruth saw more and more of each other, and one day there was a wedding in Bethlehem. It must have been quite an event, for Boaz was very rich and Ruth very poor, and a Moabitess too.

People must have talked about it for weeks, and they would have talked still more if they had known what would come of it in the years ahead. For Ruth and Boaz had a son called Obed. And Obed had a son called Jesse. And Jesse had a son called David.

So Ruth, dear, kind, faithful Ruth, was the great-grand-mother of King David, the great-great-grandmother of King Solomon, and a direct ancestor of Joseph, husband of Mary who, a thousand years later, in this selfsame village of Bethlehem, gave birth to the baby Jesus.

I am sure Ruth never dreamed so great an honor would be hers when, away in her native Moab, she listened to Naomi telling those wonderful stories of the God of Israel, the God of heaven and earth. How glad she will be, through all eternity, that she gave her heart to Him then.

PART IV

Stories of Samuel and Saul

(1 SAMUEL 1:16-13:7)

STORY 1

Lent to the Lord

ALL this time the tabernacle built in the wilderness had been at Shiloh, about twenty-five miles north of Jerusalem, where Joshua had set it up shortly after crossing the Jordan. It looked pretty shabby by now, after being exposed to all kinds of weather for nearly three hundred years, but it was still the center of worship for all who were faithful to the God of heaven.

Inside it still were the ark, the seven-branched candlestick, the altar of incense, and the table of shewbread, which young Bezaleel had made with such wonderful skill. Outside was the brazen altar, green with age, with smoke rising from a sacrifice just offered upon it.

Eli was the high priest now, a very weak man, nothing like Aaron or Eleazar, who had held the office at first. His two spoiled boys, Hophni and Phinehas, were up to all kinds of mischief, and because of their bad example people visiting the tabernacle were beginning to lose all respect for the holy place.

3-10

Hannah had dedicated her son Samuel to the Lord before he was born, and now she brought him to live with the high priest Eli to be trained in the tabernacle for God's service.

As you can imagine, God was much displeased, and began to look for another leader.

One day as Eli was sitting on a seat by one of the tent posts, his attention was drawn to a woman who was acting in a very strange way. She seemed to be making faces and talking to herself, and Eli came to the conclusion that she must be drunk.

Seeing a chance to do something to stop the wickedness going on around the tabernacle, he scolded the woman severely and told her to stop drinking.

"I'm not drunk," she said. "I'm just too sad to speak. I was only pouring out my heart to God."

Now Eli was sorry he had spoken so harshly, and asked her what was the trouble.

Then Hannah told her story.

She said she was married to a kind man called Elkanah, but she didn't have a baby. And oh, how she wanted a baby! Her friends had babies, lots of them, but she didn't have one. Not a single one. It didn't seem fair.

She had cried and cried about it until she couldn't cry any more. Her husband had said to her, "Am not I better than ten sons?" but of course he didn't understand how she felt.

She had prayed again and again about it, but nothing had happened. Now she had come to the tabernacle, once more to ask God to please give her a baby, and soon. And if He should do so, she said eagerly, "I will give him to the Lord all the days of his life."

146

LENT TO THE LORD

Eli's heart was touched. "Go in peace," he said to her tenderly. "And God grant your prayer."

Hannah stopped sobbing. A beautiful smile spread over her tear-stained face.

From what Eli had said, and the way he had said it, she felt sure her prayer would be answered. She went home happy for the first time in years.

God answered her prayer. In no time at all—or so it seemed to her—a lovely baby boy arrived, and she called him Samuel.

Samuel means "asked of God," so it was very fitting that Hannah should call her precious baby by that name.

How glad she was to have a little boy all her own! What made her happier still was the thought that this dear bundle of love had come to her straight from heaven in answer to her prayers.

Next time Elkanah went up to the tabernacle at Shiloh, Hannah stayed home, the better to care for her baby. Tenderly she watched over him, day by day and month by month, treasuring every precious minute she had him with her. For she had not forgotten her promise to lend him to the Lord.

When at last Samuel was big enough to feed himself and run around on his own, she took him to Eli.

At first the old man didn't seem to recognize her, so she said, "Oh my lord, as thy soul liveth, my lord, I am the woman that stood by thee here, praying unto the Lord."

Then she pointed to little Samuel, holding tightly to her dress. "For this child I prayed," she said. "Therefore also I have lent him to the Lord; as long as he liveth he shall be lent to the Lord."

Eli was quite taken aback. He had never seen such earnestness, such devotion, such love for God, as he saw on Hannah's face at this moment. It was so different from the ugly, unkind looks he had seen so often on the faces of his sons. If only everybody in Israel would love God like this, and be willing to lend their children to Him, how different everything would be!

Reverently the old man bowed his head and worshiped.

As for Hannah, she dropped to her knees and began to pray, "My heart rejoiceth in the Lord . . . ; because I rejoice in thy salvation. There is none holy as the Lord: for there is none beside thee: neither is there any rock like our God."

This was no silent prayer, like the one she had prayed years before. Aloud she cried, for all to hear, "He raiseth up the poor out of the dust, and lifteth up the beggar from the dunghill, to set them among princes, and to make them inherit the throne of glory."

Hannah felt like a princess herself at that moment. And she knew in her heart that Samuel, her precious little Samuel, was now a prince of God. Had she not lent him to the Lord of glory for the rest of his life, indeed forever and ever?

148

STORY 2

Voice in the Night

≈≈≈≈≈≈≈≈≈≈≈≈≈

I WOULDN'T be surprised if Samuel cried himself to sleep that first night he was left alone with Eli, for he was only a little boy and had never been away from his mother before.

As for Hannah, I am sure she cried all the way home as she thought of her lonely darling in the old tabernacle, and what those two big bullies, Hophni and Phinehas, might do to him. Yet in her heart she was sure that she had done right. Had not Samuel come to her as a special gift from God? Had she not promised to lend him to the Lord?

Never for a moment did she forget her precious boy, even though God gave her three more sons and two daughters. Day by day, whenever she could get time, she worked on a little coat for him, taking it with her to Shiloh the next time she went with her husband to offer the yearly sacrifice.

What a meeting that was! Can't you see little Samuel running to her with outstretched arms, crying, "Mamma!

149

Mamma! O Mamma dear! You have come to see me at last!"

Year by year Hannah came to Shiloh, bringing a new coat with her each time. And each one was a little longer, and a little wider, as Samuel grew bigger and bigger and one birthday followed another.

All these years the little boy busied himself around the tabernacle doing all sorts of things to help Eli. No doubt there was a great deal of cleaning and polishing and clearing up needed, all jobs that a boy of Samuel's age could do so well.

He was such a nice little fellow that Eli grew to love him dearly. No doubt he told him the whole wonderful story of the tabernacle, how God had given it to His people to remind them of His own great sacrifice to save them from sin and to prepare them for the day when they could live in the Garden of Eden again.

Samuel loved to listen to the old man's tales of long ago, and must have learned much of God's dealings with His people.

Then one night something very wonderful happened.

150

VOICE IN THE NIGHT

Samuel had finished his work for the day, and had gone to his little bed. All was quiet in the tabernacle, and the flickering lamp was casting strange shadows on the walls and ceiling. Then suddenly he heard someone call his name.

"Samuel."

Thinking that Eli must want something, he jumped up and ran to the old man.

"Here I am," he said.

"I didn't call you," said Eli. "Go and lie down again."

A little while later the voice called again.

"Samuel."

Obediently Samuel got up again and ran to Eli.

"Here I am," he said. "You *did* call me."

"No, my son," said Eli. "I didn't call you. Lie down again."

Puzzled, Samuel went back to his bed. Somebody had called him, he was sure. And if not Eli, who could it be? There was nobody else around, so far as he knew.

Then he heard the voice again.

"Samuel."

Once more he ran to Eli.

"You *did* call me," he said.

Eli was puzzled now. Clearly someone had spoken to the boy. He guessed it must be God.

VOICE IN THE NIGHT

Gently he said to Samuel, "Go, lie down, and if you hear the voice again, say, Speak, Lord, for thy servant heareth."

Very excited now, Samuel hurried back to bed. But not to sleep. How could he? Instead, he lay there wide awake, listening. Would the voice speak again? And would it really be God?

Then he heard it. So gentle, kind, and tender it was, as God would speak to a little boy.

"Samuel, Samuel."

Trembling, Samuel whispered, "Speak; for thy servant heareth."

Then God told him of the trouble that was about to come to Eli because he had not trained his boys to do right, and had let them do so many wicked things around the tabernacle.

Samuel didn't sleep the rest of that night. He just lay there tossing about until the morning, wondering whether he should tell Eli what God had said to him. He loved his old master dearly, and didn't want to hurt him. But, oh dear, what was he supposed to do now God had given him such a message?

Eli settled the matter for him in the morning. He hadn't slept much that night either. Naturally he wondered why God had chosen to speak to one so young as Samuel, instead of to him, the high priest. And he was filled with curiosity to know what God had said.

"Samuel, my son," he said, as he heard the boy up and about again at break of day. "What did God say to you? Don't hide it from me."

153

When Samuel heard a gentle voice calling him in the middle of the night, he remembered what Eli the priest had told him and cried out eagerly, "Speak; for thy servant heareth."

Slowly, sadly, Samuel began to speak. Little by little he told the whole story and "hid nothing." When he was finished Eli said, "It is the Lord: let him do what seems good to him."

Nothing more happened that day, nor the next. But as Samuel went about his tasks he couldn't help thinking about that voice in the night. It was such a sweet and kindly voice, something like his mother's, which he heard so seldom now. Perhaps he would hear it again. He hoped so.

Many a night before he went to sleep he listened for it. Then he began to talk to God and wait for His answers.

How very wonderful! A little boy talking with the great God of heaven!

Soon they were fast friends.

"And Samuel grew, and the Lord was with him. And . . . the Lord revealed himself to Samuel in Shiloh."

STORY 3

Dangerous Plunder

YEARS went by. Samuel grew to manhood and became known through all Israel as a prophet of God. How proud his mother must have been of him—and how glad that she had lent him to the Lord when he was a little boy!

So far the message he had passed on to Eli from the Lord had not come true. Eli was still alive. His two sons Hophni and Phinehas were behaving worse than ever. Yet Samuel felt it could not be long before something would happen to cause God's word to be fulfilled.

One day messengers arrived at Shiloh from the camp of Israel to say they wanted to take away the ark. The army had been defeated in battle with the Philistines, and the leaders had decided that their only hope of victory was to have the sacred ark among them.

Eli did not like to see the ark taken from the holy of holies. But Hophni and Phinehas took no notice of anything he may have said. Together they carried the ark out of the tabernacle to the camp.

155

"And when the ark of the covenant of the Lord came into the camp, all Israel shouted with a great shout, so that the earth rang again." The people looked on the ark as some sort of magic charm that would bring them victory no matter what sort of lives they were living or how much evil was in their hearts.

How mistaken they were! Next day, as the Israelites went into battle again, they were slaughtered. Thirty thousand men were killed, including Hophni and Phinehas. "And the ark of God was taken."

Meanwhile up in Shiloh, Eli waited for news. He was deeply worried about his two sons, and the ark.

As he sat on a seat near the tabernacle, a man came hurrying up the steep mountain trail. His clothes were torn and there was earth on his head, a sign of mourning in those days. As he entered Shiloh and told his story, the people wailed aloud in sorrow.

"What meaneth the noise of this tumult?" called Eli, now ninety-eight years old, and blind. "What has gone wrong?"

Then the messenger came and told Eli all that had happened. "Israel is fled before the Philistines," he said, "and there has been also a great slaughter among the people, and your two sons also, Hophni and Phinehas, are dead, and the ark of God is taken."

As the man mentioned the ark of God, Eli fainted, and falling backward off the seat, hit his head heavily on the ground and broke his neck.

At that very moment the wife of Phinehas died also as

she gave birth to a little boy. In her last breath she called the baby "Ichabod. And she said, The glory is departed from Israel: for the ark of God is taken."

Meanwhile the Philistines carried the ark in triumph to the city of Ashdod and put it in the temple of their god Dagon. Of all the plunder they had taken from the Israelites that day, this was by far the most valuable. Not only was it overlaid with gold: it was, they thought, the secret of Israel's strength. But they soon found it was a most dangerous piece of booty.

They thought their victory proved that their famous idol was greater than the God of Israel, but next morning Dagon was found lying face down in the earth before the ark. An angel must have pushed it over in the night.

The Philistines set Dagon up in his place again, but next morning he was down on the floor once more, this time all broken to pieces. His head and his hands had been snapped off and left in the doorway, fairly frightening the priests out of their wits when they arrived to open the temple in the morning.

What could have happened to their god? they wondered. Who could have smashed him to bits like this?

They were still wondering when a lot of people in the town suddenly became very ill. So many died of a strange disease that the leading men of Ashdod got together and decided that they must get rid of the ark of God at once. They felt sure it was the cause of all their trouble. So they sent the ark to the city of Gath.

No sooner had the ark been brought to Gath, however, than the same disease broke out there. More and more people became sick and died. So the people of Gath decided to send the ark to Ekron, and the same thing happened there.

After seven months of this the Philistines had had enough. Everywhere the people were saying to their leaders, "Send away the ark of the God of Israel, and let it go again to his own place, that it slay us not."

At last the five lords of the Philistines agreed to act. They called for the priests of Dagon and asked what they should do. These men advised that the ark be put upon a new cart, drawn by two cows, and set on the road to the city of Beth-shemesh in the land of Israel.

If the cows should leave their calves behind, they said, and follow the road all the way to Beth-shemesh, then it would be clear that the Philistines had done the right thing and that all their trouble had come upon them because they had kept the ark.

A lot of people watched that cart as it set off, and no one was sorry to see it go. You can imagine their thoughts as they saw the two cows, without any driver, go straight along the highway, "lowing as they went" and turning not aside "to the right hand or to the left."

More interested than anybody else were the five lords of the Philistines. They followed right behind the cart, eager to see what would happen to it. And they could hardly believe their eyes as they saw those two cows pull the cart, uphill, clear into the land of Israel.

How wonderful is the power of the God of heaven! they must have thought.

STORY 4

An Unheeded Warning

WHEN Hophni and Phinehas rashly took the ark away from the holy of holies, they did more damage than they knew. That day the glory departed not only from Israel but from the tabernacle too. The ark never got back to Shiloh.

With the ark gone, and Eli dead, Samuel returned to his old home at Ramah, where, for all we know, his mother may still have been alive. She had lent him to the Lord, and now he was back again, a strong, wise leader of His people.

Samuel built a house in Ramah and married. And from here he went out all over Israel calling the people to turn from their sins and worship the God of heaven, who had delivered them from Egypt and brought them into the land of Canaan. "And he went from year to year in circuit to Bethel, and Gilgal, and Mizpeh, and judged Israel in all those places."

During all these years there was trouble between Israel and the Philistines, but Samuel kept saying that if the people

would but turn to the Lord with all their hearts, and put away the strange gods from among them, and serve Him only, all would be well. They would never need to fear the Philistines any more.

Once when he had called a meeting at Mizpeh, word spread that the Philistines were on their way with a large army. Everybody was frightened, but Samuel went on with the service, praying to God for deliverance. Suddenly there was a tremendous burst of thunder from the skies. The Philistines scattered, and the Israelites chased them clear to the border. Samuel set up a stone as a monument of the great deliverance and called it Ebenezer, saying, "Hitherto hath the Lord helped us."

Thanks to Samuel's able leadership "the Philistines were subdued, and they came no more into the coast of Israel." The Israelites even recaptured such important cities as Ekron and Gath.

One day, when Samuel was getting old, the elders of Israel came to Ramah to see him. They were worried about what would happen after his death. For, alas, Samuel had done no better in bringing up his sons than Eli had with Hophni and Phinehas. He had been so busy preaching and traveling that he hadn't taken time to train his boys aright, and now they were giving him a lot of trouble and disappointment. He had hoped that one of them, at least, might take his place when he died, but it was not to be. None of them was good enough, and everybody knew it.

"You are getting old," said the elders, "and your sons are not like you; now make us a king to judge us like all the nations."

Samuel was shocked. A king! Israel had never had any king but God. Had He not been to them far more than a king ever since He brought them out of Egypt? Why should they want a king now?

Samuel was so displeased that he left the elders and went away by himself to ask God what to do.

God told Samuel to do what the people wanted, and not to take their request as an insult to himself, "for they have not rejected thee," He said, "but they have rejected me, that I should not reign over them."

Samuel went back to the elders and warned them what would happen if they insisted on having a king.

"He will take your sons," he said, "and appoint them for himself, for his chariots, and to be his horsemen . . . and to make his instruments of war. . . . And he will take your daughters to be confectionaries, and to be cooks, and to be bakers. And he will take your fields, and your vineyards, and your oliveyards, even the best of them, and give them to his servants. . . . And he will take . . . your goodliest young men, and your asses, and put them to work."

How true were his words! But the elders would not heed his warning. They got angry. "Nay!" they cried, "but we *will* have a king over us; that we also may be like all the nations; and that our king may judge us, and go out before us, and fight our battles."

There was no way to change their minds. They were sure that a king was all they needed to get them out of their troubles. They were wrong, hopelessly wrong, but they couldn't see it. They had to learn by experience.

When Samuel told the Lord what the elders had said, God told him to do what they wanted. "Make them a king," He said.

So the elders went back to their homes, and Samuel began to search for a young man who might be worthy to be the first king of Israel.

STORY 5

Choosing a King

WHAT would you do if you were asked to find someone to be a king? Where would you look for him? What kind of person would he be?

This was Samuel's problem. The elders of Israel had said, "Give us a king!" Now it was up to him to find one.

No doubt he thought of all the fine young men he had met on his travels through the country. There was that big, strapping fellow he had seen in a meeting at Gilgal, but no, he wasn't good enough. There was that nice-looking lad in a home he had visited at Bethel, but he wasn't strong enough. Yet somewhere there must be a young man who would be just right for the job, but who was he, and where?

Then one day God told Samuel that he wouldn't have to search any more. The young man was on his way to him and would arrive in the city the next morning. "Tomorrow about this time," He said, "I will send thee a man out of the land of Benjamin, and thou shalt anoint him to be captain over my people Israel."

164

Early next morning Samuel went to the city gate and watched everybody who came in. As the people streamed by he wondered whether this man or that was the right one. One of them would be the first king of Israel. But which one would it be?

Then his eyes rested upon one of the finest young men he had ever seen, a "choice young man and goodly." Tall, handsome, and powerfully built, he stood out among the crowd as if born to be a leader.

As this splendid youth, standing head and shoulders above everybody around, came toward Samuel, God said to the prophet, "Behold the man. . . . This same shall reign over my people."

Of course the young man, whose name was Saul, did not know anything about this. In fact, he had never seen Samuel before. For the past three days he had been searching for his father's lost asses, and those asses were all that concerned him at the moment. His servant had suggested that maybe the seer

165

who lived in this city could tell where the asses could be found, and that's why he had come.

"Is the seer here?" Saul asked.

"I am the seer," said Samuel. "And don't worry about the asses that were lost three days ago; they have been found."

How does he know about my father's asses? wondered Saul. How could he possibly have heard that they have been found? For, of course, there was no telegraph or telephone in those days.

Then Samuel invited Saul and his servant to dine at his house. When they were shown into the parlor they found about thirty people there, and you can imagine Saul's surprise when he and his servant were given the most honored seats. He was still more surprised when Samuel told his cook to bring the special portion of food he had reserved for this occasion and set it before him.

Everybody in the room must have wondered why the stranger was treated so well. Perhaps, some thought, it was because he had just come to town, or that he was related to Samuel in some way, or that he was such a big man he needed extra food. But Samuel never said a word. He just let them think what they pleased. Someday they would find out.

That evening Samuel and Saul had a long talk together under the stars on the flat roof of his house. Then they went to bed.

Next morning the prophet walked with Saul and his servant to the outskirts of the city to bid them good-by. There he whispered to Saul, "Tell your servant to walk on ahead."

CHOOSING A KING

The servant obeyed. Then Samuel opened a small bottle of oil he had brought with him and poured it upon Saul's head. After that he kissed him and said he was now anointed to be captain of the Lord's people.

Something happened to Saul at that moment. As he turned to go from Samuel "God gave him another heart." That means that all his thoughts and plans were changed. Up to this moment he had thought only of himself; now he began to think about others and what he must do for his people and his God.

Samuel told him that when he should arrive at Rachel's tomb he would meet two men who would tell him that his father's asses were found. Then in the plain of Tabor he would meet three men—one carrying three kids, one carrying three loaves of bread, and another carrying a bottle of wine. They would give him two loaves of bread. Then when he got to the "hill of God" he would meet a company of prophets, singing and prophesying, and he would join them.

Everything happened exactly as Samuel had said, which helped Saul to believe that everything else the prophet had told

him was equally true. Then, some days later, he went to Mizpeh.

Thousands of people were gathered there, and Saul guessed that this was the time when Samuel would present him as their king. He began to be afraid, and hid himself among the baggage.

From where he lay he could hear Samuel speaking to the people, reminding them of all God had done for Israel since He had brought them out of Egypt.

Then he heard lots being cast to discover the tribe in which the new king would be found. Perhaps the tribe of Judah would be taken, he thought, or maybe the tribe of Simeon. He hoped so, for that would let him out.

But no. The tribe of Benjamin was taken. His tribe.

Then lots were cast among the families of Benjamin, then

among members of the family of Kish. Finally his name was called.

"Saul! Saul!" cried his friends. But he didn't answer. The great moment of his life had come and he was not ready for it. Instead he was hiding behind a heap of bedding or maybe a pile of pots and pans or a bale of hay. And there at last they found him.

Led by an excited group to Samuel, he turned and faced the crowd, just as the prophet said, "See ye him whom the Lord hath chosen, that there is none like him among all the people."

Saul would gladly have run away, back to his farm, anywhere, but he couldn't; and suddenly a great shout went up, "God save the king! God save the king!"

STORY 6

Saul Saves the People's Eyes

NOT all the people of Israel were happy about the choice of Saul to be king. Some turned up their noses and said, "How shall this man save us?"

Meanwhile Saul went back home and worked on his farm as usual. Here was one king who had no palace, no parliament, no army, no police force. Many times he must have wondered what a king was supposed to do.

Then one day as he was driving a herd of cattle out of a field, news reached him that the Ammonites had surrounded Jabesh-gilead and threatened to put out the right eyes of all the people in the city.

Here was a challenge, and Saul rose to it. Now he knew what a king should do. Quickly he sent messengers throughout all Israel, calling for volunteers to go with him to save the citizens of Jabesh-gilead from the cruel Ammonites.

There was a wonderful response. The people came as one man—three hundred and thirty thousand of them. And they came quickly, all ready for battle.

SAUL SAVES THE PEOPLE'S EYES

Saul's spirits rose at sight of this mighty army, and he told the messengers from Jabesh-gilead to hurry home and say to their frightened friends, "Tomorrow, by that time the sun be hot, ye shall have help."

All that night the men of Israel marched, with Saul proudly leading them. Then in the morning watch they came upon the Ammonites and, taking them completely by surprise, defeated them so thoroughly that "two of them were not left together."

So Jabesh-gilead was delivered, and Saul saved the people's eyes.

Everybody was so happy about this victory—the first under Saul's leadership—that some asked, "Who is he that said, Shall Saul reign over us? bring the men, that we may put them to death."

"No, no," said Saul. "There shall not a man be put to death this day: for to day the Lord hath wrought salvation in Israel."

In all this Samuel saw a wonderful chance to give Saul a better start as the new king. So he suggested that all the people make their way to Gilgal and "renew the kingdom there." This they did. The tens of thousands who had answered Saul's call to save Jabesh-gilead, now moved on Gilgal, flushed with the spirit of victory. There, though they had chosen him to be king before, they made him king again amid great rejoicing.

Samuel offered sacrifices, and the people ate and drank to their heart's content. Things hadn't looked so good for a long time.

"Behold the king whom ye have chosen, and whom ye have desired!" he said to the vast assembly.

"If ye will fear the Lord, and serve him, and obey his voice, and not rebel against the commandment of the Lord,

then shall both ye and also the king that reigneth over you continue following the Lord your God: But if ye will not obey the voice of the Lord, . . . then shall the hand of the Lord be against you, as it was against your fathers."

Earnestly he pleaded with them, "Turn not aside from following the Lord, but serve the Lord with all your heart. . . . For the Lord will not forsake his people for his great name's sake: because it hath pleased the Lord to make you his people. . . . Only fear the Lord, and serve him in truth with all your heart: for consider how great things he hath done for you."

At that moment everybody wanted to do right and serve the Lord with all their heart forever. Alas, how quickly they forgot their good resolutions! How soon they were in trouble again!

173

STORY 7

The Price of Impatience

S AUL had reigned less than two years when things began
to go wrong again.

Out of all the men who had answered his call to
fight the Ammonites, he had kept three thousand as a sort of
bodyguard, and sent the rest home. Then he had put one thousand of these under the command of his son Jonathan.

Being young and headstrong, Jonathan stirred up trouble
with the Philistines by attacking one of their garrisons. In
revenge the Philistines gathered a huge army of thirty thousand chariots and six thousand horsemen, and "people as the
sand which is on the sea shore," and marched against Israel.

When news of this new invasion reached the Israelites,
they were scared to death. They hid "in caves, and in thickets,
and in rocks, and in high places, and in pits." Many fled across
the Jordan for safety. "As for Saul, he was yet in Gilgal, and
all the people followed him trembling."

Samuel had said he would meet Saul there within seven

days, but day after day went by, and he did not turn up. Meanwhile more and more men left Saul and fled. By the seventh day his bodyguard had dwindled to only six hundred.

The young king became very impatient. Why had not Samuel kept his promise? Surely he knew how serious the situation had become. Soon there would be no army left at all.

Suddenly he made up his mind. He wouldn't wait for Samuel any longer. He would offer the burnt offering in Samuel's place. And why not? After all, wasn't he king?

So he killed the animal that was to be offered as a sacrifice, and burned it on the altar.

Hardly had the smoke blown away, however, when "behold, Samuel came."

Saul hurried to greet him, but there was a grieved look on the old man's face.

"What have you done?" he said.

Saul did his best to explain. "Because the people were scattering, and you didn't come, and the Philistines were getting nearer, well, I forced myself therefore, and offered a burnt offering."

"Thou hast done foolishly!" said Samuel sternly. "Thou hast not kept the commandment of the Lord thy God, which he commanded thee."

By failing to wait for Samuel, and by taking it upon himself to offer a burnt offering, which he was not supposed to do, Saul had revealed serious weaknesses in his character. He had shown that he wasn't the sort of man Samuel had thought he was. He wasn't wise enough or good enough to be a king, for he didn't know how to obey.

"Thy kingdom shall not continue," warned the prophet. Then, as a parting thrust, he added, "The Lord hath sought him a man after his own heart, and the Lord hath commanded him to be captain over his people."

It was a hard thing to say at such a time, but no doubt Saul needed it.

A moment later Samuel was gone, and Saul was left on his own—with only six hundred men to face the might of the advancing Philistines.

Looking at the dying embers of the sacrifice he had offered, he wished he hadn't been so rash. And he wondered if God had really forsaken him so soon.

Discouraged, he moved his faithful band of followers to as safe a place as possible in "the uttermost part of Gibeah," and set up his headquarters under a pomegranate tree.

Many a time he must have wished he had never gone looking for his father's asses. Then he would never have met Samuel, and never would have been made king. And he wouldn't have got into this dreadful fix.

What to do next he did not know. Israel's cause looked hopeless. What could he do with but six hundred men?

176

STORY 8

Brave Young Prince

≋≋≋≋≋≋≋≋≋≋≋≋≋≋≋≋≋≋≋≋≋≋

THERE was at least one person on Saul's side who was not discouraged, and that was Jonathan. He knew all about the thirty thousand chariots and the six thousand horsemen the Philistines had, and how few were the men who had stayed by his father. Yet he was sure God could still save Israel, if He would.

One day, without saying a word to his father, he slipped out of the camp with his armorbearer and made his way through a rocky pass toward the army of the Philistines.

"Come," he said to his armorbearer, "it may be that the Lord will work for us: for there is no restraint to the Lord to save by many or by few."

That was a grand thing for him to say; and God loves young people with such faith and courage.

Together the two young men crept from boulder to boulder until they were almost within shouting distance of a Philistine outpost on the top of a steep cliff.

As the armorbearer was wondering what Jonathan would do next, the young prince whispered to him, "We will let them see us; and if they say, 'Wait till we come to you,' then we will not go up to them. But if they say, 'Come up unto us,' then we will go up, for the Lord has delivered them into our hand: and this shall be a sign unto us."

So they stepped out from behind a boulder and shouted to the men above them.

"Look!" cried the Philistine soldiers with a sneer, "the Hebrews come forth out of the holes where they had hid themselves."

Seeing there were but two young men in the valley they said, "Come up to us, and we will show you a thing."

This was the sign Jonathan had been waiting for. "Come up after me," he said to his armorbearer as he started to climb toward the top of the cliff.

The Philistines were taken completely by surprise. For they never expected the two young men to fight—not after climbing all the way up so steep a cliff. But they didn't know Jonathan or his armorbearer.

Drawing their swords, the two young men struck down about twenty men.

Just at that moment, in the midst of the fighting, there was a great earthquake. The very mountains seemed to tremble. Panic seized the Philistines. They began to fight one another.

By this time Saul's watchmen at Gibeah had noticed that something had gone wrong in the camp of the Philistines. The mighty host seemed to be melting away as "they went on beating down one another."

Courage came back to the little band of six hundred men. As quickly as they could they ran toward the struggling mass of humanity, where "every man's sword was against his fellow."

More and more Israelites came out of their hiding places and joined in the battle. When the Philistines saw them coming they started to run, and the Israelites won a very great victory.

"So the Lord saved Israel that day"—through the faith and bravery of Jonathan and his armorbearer.

But Saul had done another foolish thing, which spoiled everything. For some unknown reason he had said to his soldiers as they went into battle, "Cursed be the man who eats

179

any food until evening." So, hungry as they were, the soldiers ate nothing all that day.

Some of them, as they pursued the Philistines, came to a forest and found a large honeycomb "upon the ground," perhaps in a hollow tree. How good it looked! But they didn't dare touch it lest Saul should put them to death.

At that moment Jonathan came on the scene and caught sight of the honey. Since he had not heard his father's order not to eat, he went right ahead and ate some of the honey.

"There'll be trouble about this," warned one of the men who saw him do it, but Jonathan laughed it off. He couldn't see why people shouldn't eat on a day like this. "Just see how much better I am for eating," he said jokingly, remarking that the victory might have been very much bigger if only everybody else had eaten some honey too!

Trouble came soon enough. Though nobody told Saul what Jonathan had done, rumor reached him that somebody had eaten food that day, and he swore that he would find out who it was.

So angry did he become that someone had disobeyed him that he quite forgot this was a day of triumph, when everyone should be happy and thankful, and he vowed that he would kill the culprit even if it were his own son.

Then he called all his men together and told them that they would be on one side, and he and Jonathan on the other side. After that he ordered lots to be cast between the two sides. This was done. And you can imagine his surprise when the lot fell upon himself and Jonathan.

You could have heard a pin drop at that moment.

Then Saul ordered, "Cast lots between me and Jonathan my son." Again the lots were cast, and Jonathan was taken.

Now Saul was really in a difficult spot.

"What have you done?" he asked sternly, while everyone looking on held his breath.

"I did but taste a little honey," said Jonathan meekly, "and, lo, I must die."

His pride hurt, Saul said angrily, "God do so and more also: for thou shalt surely die, Jonathan."

Then a glorious thing happened. A roar of protest rose from the people. "No!" they cried. "Shall Jonathan die, who hath wrought this great salvation in Israel? God forbid: as the Lord liveth there shall not one hair of his head fall to the ground; for he hath wrought with God this day.

"So the people rescued Jonathan."

STORY 9

Obedience, Not Sacrifice

NOT far from the land of Israel lived a people called the Amalekites. So wicked had they become that God said that they must be destroyed. Just as, long before, He had had to send fire from heaven to burn up Sodom and Gomorrah, so now He sent Israel to blot out the Amalekites. These people were so bad that there was no hope they would ever repent of their sins.

Samuel brought God's message to Saul and told him to "go and smite Amalek, and utterly destroy all that they have."

This was not to be an ordinary war, but a divine punishment. No spoil of any kind was to be taken. Nothing was to be spared, not even the animals. Even they might be diseased as a result of the wrongdoing of these sinful people.

Saul understood perfectly well what he was to do. It wasn't a pleasant task, but as God had ordered him to do it, he made plans to carry it out. Once again he sent messengers through the land of Israel, calling men to join his army. Two hundred and ten thousand men answered his call this time.

The Amalekites didn't have a chance against so many. They were completely wiped out. Only Agag their king was taken alive—and "the best of the sheep, and of the oxen, and of the fatlings, and the lambs."

All the worthless animals were destroyed, but those that looked strong and healthy—well, it seemed too bad to kill them too. After all, they were very valuable. Good animals were scarce.

So the two hundred and ten thousand men marched back from Amalek driving hundreds of sheep and oxen before them. They looked like an army bringing back the spoils of battle.

Saul was feeling very pleased with himself. A nasty job had been done. The people were happy with the loot they had won. They had food for a long time to come. All in all everything had turned out very well indeed. Surely Samuel would be very glad and grateful when he heard the story.

But Samuel was neither glad nor grateful.

As the old prophet came into the camp, Saul, all smiles, hurried over to greet him.

"Blessed be thou of the Lord," he said. "I have performed the commandment of the Lord."

"So!" said Samuel, looking at him sternly. "Then what is the meaning of the bleating of the sheep and the lowing of the oxen which I hear?"

"Oh, that," said Saul, ever ready with an excuse. "They have brought them from the Amalekites: for the people spared the best of the sheep and of the oxen, to sacrifice unto the Lord; and the rest we have utterly destroyed."

"Stop!" cried Samuel. "I will tell you what the Lord told me last night."

"Say on," said Saul.

"When you were little in your own sight," said Samuel, "were you not made the head of the tribes of Israel, and the Lord anointed you king over Israel? And the Lord sent you

184

on a journey, and said, 'Go and utterly destroy the sinners the Amalekites.' Why then did you not obey the voice of the Lord, but flew upon the spoil and did evil in the sight of the Lord?"

"But," said Saul, "I have obeyed the voice of the Lord, and have gone the way which the Lord sent me. But the people took of the spoil, sheep and oxen, the chief of the things which should have been utterly destroyed, to sacrifice unto the Lord in Gilgal."

"Has the Lord as great delight in burnt offerings and sacrifices," asked Samuel, "as in obeying the voice of the Lord? Behold, to obey is better than sacrifice, and to hearken than the fat of rams."

Then he added these solemn words: "Because you have rejected the word of the Lord, he has rejected you from being king."

Rejected!

Saul was shocked. He had never thought that anything like that would happen. And all over a few sheep and oxen! Surely God would not take the kingdom from him over a little point like that!

Alas, he had not learned how important obedience is in the sight of God.

"Pardon my sin," he cried, begging for another chance.

But it was too late.

Samuel merely repeated what he had said before, "The Lord has rejected you from being king over Israel."

As the prophet turned to leave, Saul grabbed his garment, as though to keep him there, and the garment tore.

185

Looking at the tear, Samuel said, "The Lord has rent the kingdom of Israel from you this day, and given it to a neighbor of yours, who is better than you."

So there was no hope. None.

Saul was heartbroken. How foolish he had been! What a price he had to pay for his folly!

That night, as he lay in his tent listening to the bleating of the sheep and the lowing of the oxen he should have destroyed, he no doubt repeated to himself, over and over again, those striking words Samuel had said to him, "To obey is better than sacrifice, and to hearken than the fat of rams."

To obey . . . to obey . . . to obey.

Thus he learned, too late, that obedience, not sacrifice, is what God wants most from us all.

STORY 10

God Finds Another Boy

AS SAUL lay there in his tent that night thinking about all that Samuel had told him, he began to wonder what the prophet could have meant when he said that the kingdom would be taken from him and given to a neighbor of his, someone who was better than he.

A neighbor! he thought. Which neighbor?

His mind ran over all the people he knew—the man who ran the farm next to his, or one of the abler men in his army, or Jonathan. Yes, what about Jonathan? Was he going to be punished because of his father's sin?

Try as he would, Saul could find no answer to his questions. If God was looking for another king, he hadn't given a hint as to who it might be. That is, not to Saul.

But he had to Samuel.

"Go to the home of Jesse, of Bethlehem," God had said to him. "For I have found a king among his sons."

When Samuel arrived at Jesse's home he soon discovered

187

that he had a bigger problem than he had expected. For Jesse had many sons, all of them tall, strong, handsome young fellows. How was he to tell which one God had in mind to be the next king of Israel?

Of course Samuel didn't tell anybody why he had come. That wouldn't have been wise. Instead he said he had come to offer a sacrifice, and everybody in town believed that was the only reason he was there.

After the sacrifice Samuel asked Jesse to introduce his sons to him, and he was very happy to do so.

First was Eliab, the eldest. So tall and good looking was he that Samuel felt sure this was the lad he was to anoint. But as he was reaching in his pocket for his vessel of oil, God told him not to look at the young man's face or height, "be-

cause I have refused him: for the Lord sees not as man sees; for man looks on the outward appearance, but the Lord looks on the heart."

Just why God refused to take Eliab the Bible does not say. There must have been some weakness in his character that made him unfit to be a king. His father and mother did not know of it, nor his brothers, nor his friends. But God knew, and that was enough.

Then Jesse called his second son, Abinadab. But as Samuel greeted him warmly, God whispered that he hadn't chosen this lad either.

Next came Shammah, and the same thing happened again.

Jesse then brought his fourth son, his fifth, his sixth, and his seventh. But as the boys were introduced God kept saying

to Samuel, "Not this one," "Not this one," "Not this one."

By this time Samuel was really puzzled. God had refused all seven of Jesse's sons, and, so far as he could see, there were no more. What could be the matter? Had he made a mistake? Should he look them all over again?

Then he got a bright idea.

"Jesse," he said, "are these all your sons?"

"Well, no," said Jesse. "There is still the youngest. He is out caring for the sheep."

"Send and fetch him," said Samuel, all excited now. Surely, he thought, this must be the boy God had in mind. Eagerly he waited for him to come.

Meanwhile, out on the rolling hills, young David lay on his back looking up at the white fleecy clouds chasing each other across a bright blue sky. As he hummed softly to himself his father's sheep quietly nibbled the short grass all around him, their gentle bleating adding to the peacefulness of the scene.

Suddenly the stillness was broken by a distant shout. "David! David!"

David jumped to his feet. Someone was calling his name. It was one of his father's trusted servants.

"I'm over here. What do you want?"

The servant came running up the hill, panting.

"What's the matter?" asked David.

"Your father wants you at once. Samuel is here."

"Samuel? Not the prophet Samuel?"

"Yes. He is staying to dinner, and he wants to see you."

"To see me? Oh no! Why would he want to see me?"

191

As soon as the prophet Samuel saw David's smile and the goodness that shone out of his beautiful eyes, he knew that this was the boy God had chosen to be anointed king of Israel.

"But he does, and your father says you are to come at once."

Just what David did with the sheep we are not told. Perhaps the servant stayed to care for them. Anyhow, like the obedient boy he was, he ran home as fast as he could, wondering all the way what in the world was happening and why the great prophet Samuel, of all people, wanted to see him.

There was no time to clean up. Jesse hurried him right into the presence of Samuel.

Scared at having to meet such a famous man, David blushed all over. But his kindly smile, his friendly bearing, and the goodness that shone out of his beautiful eyes won Samuel's heart at once. At the same instant the prophet heard God say, "Arise, anoint him: for this is he."

Without a word Samuel took his vessel of oil and poured it on David's head.

From that moment everything was different. Though Samuel had said nothing about what God was planning for David, Jesse and his wife were sure that some great destiny lay ahead of their youngest son. The seven older boys must have had the same idea about their little brother. As for David, though he went back to caring for his father's sheep, "the Spirit of the Lord" came upon him "from that day forward."

God had found another boy. Someday, if he was good enough, wise enough, true enough, he would be king of Israel.

Russ Harlan